Sandra's Wine Life

Sandra's Wine Life
Find Your Wine Identity

Sandra Guibord

White River Press
Amherst, Massachusetts

Published by White River Press
Amherst, Massachusetts • whiteriverpress.com

ISBNs: 978-1-935052-82-1 (hardcover)
        978-1-935052-85-2 (paperback)

Book cover and interior designed by Lufkin Graphic Designs
Norwich, Vermont • www.LufkinGraphics.com

Photo credits:
Photos on pages 2, 4, 6–8, 28–30, 41, 43, 49, 55, 56, 58–60, 63, 68, 71, 84, 87, 88, 96, 107 by John Fortunato, Fortunato Photography, johnfortunato.com
Photo on page 32 by Meghan Pymm, MissMohr.com
Photo on page 110 by Chase Muller

The author and publisher specifically disclaim all responsibility for any liability, loss, or risk, personal or otherwise, which is incurred as a consequence, directly or indirectly, of the use and application of any of the contents of the book.

Library of Congress Cataloging-in-Publication Data

Names: Guibord, Sandra, 1967- author.
Title: Sandra's wine life : find your wine identity / Sandra Guibord.
Description: Amherst, Massachusetts : White River Press, 2022.
    Summary: "Wine expert Sandra Guibord shares her extensive
    knowledge to help you find your own wine identity. With Sandra by your
    side, you will become confident with your wine choices, learn how to
    pair with food, and which wines best match the season with their foods
    and occasions. Includes photos, recipes, and quizzes"-- Provided by
    publisher.
Identifiers: LCCN 2021060589 | ISBN 9781935052821 (hardcover)
Subjects: LCSH: Wine and wine making--Popular works. | Food and wine
    pairing. | Cooking (Wine)
Classification: LCC TP548 .G79 2022 | DDC 641.2/2--dc23/eng/20211230
LC record available at https://lccn.loc.gov/2021060589

*This book is inspired by my wonderful family
and friends, my beautiful sons, Chase and Brice
. . . and . . . my Barry.*

Dear Wine Friends,

WELCOME. I'm thrilled that you have picked up this book to join me on this journey. I have been fortunate enough to have spent a large portion of my career writing about wine, and presenting on television and in front of large corporations. I feel honored to share my knowledge and experiences with you.

This book is a call to action designed to get you motivated to break out of your "wine rut." That's when you know exactly where your favorite bottle is at the liquor store, and you don't take the time to explore and discover anything new. Are you someone who drinks one type of red or white wine with everything? Let's change that. I've titled this book "Wine Identity" because it is here to help you break out of that rut and enjoy new wines. When the seasons change, your wine should change, too. There's much more about this to come as you read through these pages.

I hope this book entertains you with fun stories about wine, offers interesting ideas (try my Halloween holiday candy pairings), and educates you about new varietals.

When it comes to wine, there are always questions. People often walk into a wine shop with problems to be solved. They need wine for a gift, to serve at a bridal shower, or to bring to a book club event. That's where I like to help. This book offers answers to those questions and can help you feel more confident about buying and sharing wine.

When you buy a nice bottle of wine or receive one as a gift, the first thought you may have is "I can't wait to share this," and you probably have one particular person in mind. Wine can be very personal that way. Enjoying a bottle of wine is as much about the wine itself as it is about the experience—including the environment and the people you are sharing it with.

I love to travel, and over the years, I have fallen in love with wines from different parts of the world. I've come back and shared my finds by introducing many new varietals to my family and friends. I can remember sipping wine and instantly thinking about the person I knew who would love this. The more I have learned about wine, the more I've learned about the stories of regions, the vineyards, and the many varieties of grapes. Turns out, people love to hear these stories! A little bit of wine knowledge can go a long way for you. I offer interesting facts and stories that can make you feel a bit surer of yourself on a first date or that can become a conversation starter at a cocktail party. As you read through this book, I hope you will agree that knowledge about wine is both useful and just plain entertaining.

Experiences with wine can also remind you of different times of your life. Remember that great bottle you shared on a special trip you took? How about the perfect wine that matched the meal you had with friends or family? A particular wine can represent a moment and trigger a memory. That's what makes it so personal. Throughout this book I've also shared some of my favorite family recipes that go great with wine, a few of my travel stories, and some fun wine experiments that I challenge you to try.

People always ask me what my favorite wine is. The truth is, I eat and entertain differently in July than in January, so my favorite wines change as the seasons change!

I want to teach you not to limit yourself. So, let's discover your Wine Identity and learn which wines best match the seasons with their foods and occasions.

Cheers!

Sandra

Contents

What's Your Wine Identity?. 1

Seasons:
      Spring 3
      Summer 31
      Fall. 61
      Winter 89

Sandra's Sipping Quiz for Book Clubs! 117
      Answer Key 119

Acknowledgments 125

What's Your "Wine Identity?"

WHETHER YOU KNOW IT OR NOT, you already have your own "Wine Identity." That's how you define yourself as a wine consumer. When most people walk into a wine shop, they know what they want; they tend to stick with a wine that feels familiar and "safe." But the truth is, when the seasons change, your wine choices should change, too.

Most of us eat very differently in July than we do in January. We dress in different colors, we taste an array of different cuisine. So why stick with one wine? My goal is to get people to try new things. There's so much out there. I don't want my readers to be intimidated by wine. This book is organized to help you discover your wine identity by trying new wines throughout the seasons; I hope you will use it as your portal to new wine experiences.

Sandra

Spring

SPRING IS THE TIME for everything new—new wardrobes, new romance, new opportunities, new reasons for entertaining.

Are you ready for fresh spring wines? Whether you're planning a bridal shower or brunch with the girls (see Bubble Bar!), or perhaps an elaborate (or informal) Easter or Passover gathering, the right wines guarantee a memorable event that your guests will enjoy. Select your favorites from those I've compiled, or use them to create a custom wine tasting for your friends. Spring is also the time for your creative spirit to take root and grow. Let's get creative with your wine identity and learn about new wines to enjoy this spring.

Spectrum of Spring Wines

WHITES

Prosecco

Riesling

Sauvignon Blanc/Sancerre

Grüner Veltliner

Falanghina

REDS

Pinot Noir

Grenache/Garnacha

Cabernet Franc

White Wines

PROSECCO *(ITALY)*

PROSECCO, a product of northeastern Italy, is the country's number one sparkling wine. It is made predominantly from the Glera grape, which is required by law in that region. What you might not know is that Glera isn't the only grape allowed in Prosecco wine. It's possible to blend up to 15 percent of the region's other indigenous grapes, including names like Bianchetta, Verdiso, and Perera—quite rare indeed. This 15 percent allows for each vineyard to design its own custom flavor profile for its particular Prosecco. Allowing these vineyards to play with this 15 percent gives them the creative license to push and pull the flavors to customize their wine.

Most Prosecco wines are produced in a dry, brut style. However, due to the grapes' fruity flavors of green apple, honeydew melon, pear, and honeysuckle, the wine usually seems sweeter than it is. Even though brut is the most popular sweetness level of Prosecco sold in today's market, you can find styles that are sweeter if you seek them out.

Super food-friendly, Prosecco is a sparkling wine that goes great with antipasto, cured meats, and almonds.

Surprisingly versatile, it pairs well with a wide range of cuisine genres and dishes. It can be served as an aperitif (before food), but it also works well with the main entrée. Because of its sweet aromatics and bubbles, Prosecco matches well with spicy curries and Southeast Asian fare such as Thai, Vietnamese, Hong Kong, and Singaporean cuisine. The ideology behind pairing Prosecco is to use it as a palate cleanser alongside medium-intensity foods (chicken, tofu, shrimp, or pork dishes). And to savor every sip!

Best when served at 45°F.

Originally, any sparkling wine was presented in a fluted glass. But times have changed. Do not hesitate to serve your sparkling wines in a white wine glass because the larger bowl allows the aromatics to better reach your nose.

Bubble Bar!

Baby Showers, Bridal Showers, Bachelorette Parties, Brunch, Gender Reveal Parties, or for no reason whatsoever! Bubble Bars are the perfect venue for intimate, fun events. Simply start with Prosecco (or another bubbly), set up the festive bar, offer suggestions, and let your guests customize their own dazzling bubbles!

BUBBLE BAR INGREDIENTS SUGGESTIONS *(BE CREATIVE!)*

- Mulled lemon peel, mint, and sugar
- Mint leaves
- Raspberries
- Lime slices
- Lemon peels
- Cassis and Peach Liquor

Baby Blue and Baby Pink Sparkling Cocktails

Sugar-rim the glasses and decorate with slim satin ribbon for the absolute perfect precious touch!

- Blue: a drizzle of Blue Curaçao, one part Lemonade, and two parts Prosecco
- Pink: one part Pink Lemonade and two parts Prosecco

Brunch at Darlene's House

Back when I was living in LA, my friend Darlene and I would throw fabulous brunches, and one turned out to be epic. I mean, this was a brunch that went on for ten hours. We had so much fun inventing a new cocktail that day, we named it the "Darlini" in honor of our friend. One of the women in attendance was a manager at the famed Mezzaluna ristorante. She added the Darlini to the menu at the restaurant. Rumor had it that when Hillary Clinton visited this restaurant, she was known to order the Darlini!

HOW TO MAKE A DARLINI:

- Fill a glass ¾ with Prosecco, a splash of orange juice, a splash of peach schnapps, and a couple of crushed raspberries.

Prosecco vs. Champagne: What's the Difference?

Good question! Prosecco is produced by a different method from the one used to create France's signature Champagne. Unlike Prosecco that is crafted from the Glera (once called Prosecco) grape varietal and only up to 15 percent of a few other specialty indigenous grapes, Champagne can either be from a single grape or a blend of the more common Chardonnay, Pinot Noir, or Pinot Meunier.

Prosecco Is Versatile!

The Perfect Mimosa

If you love a traditional brunch, Prosecco is our top pick for a perfect mimosa. The fruitiness in this wine amplifies the citrus flavors of the orange juice, which makes it work well with brunch-style foods. By the way, a great mimosa is 2 parts sparkling wine to 1 part juice.

Bellini

The Bellini is an Italian classic. The original recipe came from Venice and was simply 2 parts Prosecco to 1 part white peach puree, with a touch of raspberry or cherry juice. It was the fruit juice that gave the creation a unique translucent pink hue. Since then, the recipe has developed a number of variations, largely because white peaches weren't always available everywhere.

You can now buy bottled peach puree[1] that's specially made for Bellinis, or you can use canned fruit to make a puree yourself.

Sparkling Margarita

I made the following recipe that I found in *Better Homes & Gardens*[2] for my friend Kristen's birthday, and it was a huge hit. Even the guys couldn't seem to get enough!

Ingredients
- 1 cup blanco tequila
- ⅔ cup lime juice
- ⅓ cup agave nectar
- 1½ cups (approx.) of sparkling wine
- lime peel strips or lime slices

Directions
In a cocktail shaker, combine half of the tequila, lime juice, and agave nectar with plenty of ice. Shake for 5 seconds and strain the mixture into three glasses. Repeat with remaining tequila, juice, and agave nectar. Top each serving with sparkling wine. Add a strip of lime peel. Add additional lime juice to taste. Makes 6 servings.

---

1   amazon.com/Funkin-White-Peach-Puree-1kg/dp/B004KQ8F0C
2   bhg.com/recipe/drinks/sparkling-margarita/

RIESLING *(GERMANY)*

Want to add a little flirtiness to your wine identity? I've always considered Riesling to be the perfect first date wine. It's fresh and light and it goes with casual food like sushi and other Asian cuisine. It's also a little lower in alcohol so you don't make a fool out of yourself! The aromatic Riesling grape was first produced in Germany's Rhine region and produces white wines that range in style from very dry to very sweet with a bouquet of orchard fruits that include nectarine, apricot, and Honeycrisp apple. You'll notice delightful fragrances such as honeycomb, jasmine, or lime. On the palate, Riesling has *high acidity*, which makes it such a fantastic food-friendly wine. I recommend the dry Rieslings to match with your favorite take-out cuisine and casual dining; the sweeter Rieslings are great with sweeter desserts.

If you're wondering what to serve with Riesling—think spice. Because of its combination of aromatics and acidity, it is the perfect accompaniment to spicy food. Strong Indian and Asian cuisines are a perfect match. Riesling is also excellent with pork, shrimp, crab, and duck.

Best when served at 45°F.

Dating way back to at least the 15th century, Riesling emerged as a popular wine throughout the valley of the Rhine River. Because the alcohol content of wine killed bacteria, it was often safer than "natural" water, so we can only imagine the great quantities of Riesling that were consumed during that time. Wine was also the tastiest way to quench thirst back then; therefore, people "quenched" all day. One legend, however, is that it was recommended that women should not taste wine before 9:00 a.m.!
Really?

SAUVIGNON BLANC/SANCERRE
(FRANCE, AMERICA, NEW ZEALAND)

The name Sauvignon Blanc loosely translates to "Wild White"—which sounds like fun, right? A popular and unmistakable white wine, Sauvignon Blanc is loved for its "green" herbal flavors and racy acidity. Its fruit flavors are lime, green apple, passion fruit, and white peach. On the nose, expect pungent, in-your-face aromas ranging from peas, asparagus, and freshly cut grass, to tropical and ripe passion fruit, grapefruit, or even mango.

Beautiful and bright, Sauv Blanc (as it's often called) grows nearly everywhere, and thus it offers a variety of styles ranging from lean to bountiful that can differ greatly from America to France to New Zealand. In America, our Sauv Blancs are highly acidic with green grass and citrus and even a touch of passion fruit. The New Zealand Sauv Blanc is an over-the-top experience of tart grapefruit and green herbs, and it has a fan base that is passionate! In France there is an area called Sancerre where they grow Sauvignon Blanc; their style is light and acidic with a softer approach than America or New Zealand.

As for food pairing, when in doubt, go green. Sauvignon Blanc makes a wonderful choice with herb-driven sauces over chicken, tofu, or fish dishes; when matched with feta or chèvre; or accompanied by Asian flavors such as those found in Thai or Vietnamese cuisine.

Best when served at 45°–50°F.

PERFECT-PAIRING SPRING RECIPE!
Sandra's Spring Asparagus Quiche with Gruyère and Cherry Tomatoes

Spring entertaining calls for quiches, frittatas, and tasty light bites. Food doesn't need to be fussy to be elegant, but you can impress your guests very simply with this recipe. I like to make things ahead so I can lay out a beautiful spread and enjoy my guests' company. Try this recipe and serve it with a crisp Rosé, a bubbly Prosecco mimosa, or a buttery Chardonnay. Add it to your buffet with bagels and lox, premade avocado toasts, fruit salad, and a crudité veggie platter. Don't feel like cooking? You can always pick up a quiche and premade platters at your local grocer. The most important thing is enjoying springtime (and wine!) together.

Ingredients

Filling:
- 2 Tbsp. butter
- 1 medium shallot, chopped (you can use ¼ white onion instead)
- 8 small cherry tomatoes, sliced in half
- 1 tsp. white vinegar
- Himalayan salt and ground black pepper
- 1 bunch (1 pound) asparagus, tough ends removed, thinly sliced on an angle
- 6 large eggs (you must beat these on a very low setting)
- 1 cup whole milk
- ¾ cup shredded Gruyère, sharp white cheddar, or cheese of choice

Crust:
- 1 frozen deep-dish pie crust, defrosted in the tin or transferred into your serving dish.

Directions

Preheat oven to 350°F, with rack in the lowest position. In a large skillet, melt butter over medium heat. Add shallots and asparagus; season with salt and pepper and a splash of vinegar. Cook, stirring occasionally until asparagus is crisp-tender. Allow this to cool.

In a large bowl, whisk together eggs, milk, and a pinch of salt and pepper.

Place pie crust on a baking sheet and prebake for 2–3 minutes. Pull out, sprinkle with cheese, top with asparagus and shallots. Pour egg mixture on top. For a beautiful presentation, decorate the top of the quiche before baking with 5 small spears of asparagus and a few tomatoes.

Wrap edges of the pie with tinfoil for the first 20 minutes of baking to keep from burning.

Remove the tinfoil and rotate the baking sheet. Bake until the center of quiche is just set, 45–50 minutes in total time. Let stand 15 minutes before serving.

Want to make a gluten-free frittata instead?

Use the recipe above but omit the pie crust and add one additional egg. Spray your pie or quiche pan generously with oil and pour in the mixture. Bake 45 minutes and cool for 5 minutes before serving. It will puff up and taste delicious.

GRÜNER VELTLINER *(AUSTRIA)*

This wine is the pride of Austria! It is a personal favorite of mine, and I love introducing people to it. Grüner Veltliner, known as "Green Wine of Veltin," is a white wine with attitude and fragrance. I love the essence of white pepper and lime with hints of bright lily. It dances on your tongue with acidity and is a terrific, food-friendly white to enjoy not only with traditional Wiener Schnitzel, but also with spring vegetables like asparagus and artichokes. If you're a Sauvignon Blanc lover and want to try something a bit more exotic and full in the mouth, try a Grüner. And if you can't remember the odd name, just think "Groovy Jetliner"! If you ask your wine shop about it, they will know exactly what you are asking for.

Best when served at 45°–46°F.

Grüner Veltliner is believed to be "autochthonous" in Austria. Autochthonous was a new word to me when I first heard it: it means that the grapes are indigenous to the area; they were not brought in and planted there. The name Veltliner comes from the town of Veltin, which was in the lower Austrian Alps but actually is now in Valtellina, a town in northern Italy. This ancient region began making Grüner Veltliner as early as the 1600s, and is also known as the original home of bresaola—air-dried, salted beef that has been aged two to three months until it's dark red; then it's sliced thinly. A little fresh Parmesan cheese with flatbread and olives is a tasty match.

VALTELLINA, ITALY.

FALANGHINA *(ITALY)*

Falanghina grapes have two unique varieties: Falanghina Beneventana—from the Campania town Benevento, known for legendary 13th century witches—and Falanghina Flegrei—from the Campania town Campi Flegrei. Flegrei means "firefields," which refers to the grapes being grown on the slopes of extinct volcanoes. The Falanghina grape is credited to have its origin in ancient Italy in the 7th century BC, though some claim to trace it back to Greece. Its name appears to have come from the Latin word *falangae*, which is the word used to describe stakes used to support vineyard grapes.

Both types of Falanghina define Campania's signature white; they are lush with peach fruit, minerals, and almond notes. The wine can have a slight pine scent, but is better known for its citrus-blossom aromas, in particular, bitter orange. On the palate Falanghina typically shows classic apple and pear flavors, depending on where the grapes were grown, with spicy or mineral notes. A great match with scallops, prawns, or clams, Falanghina is extra special when your dish is seasoned with lemon, garlic, and parsley.

Best when served at 49°–50° F.

Red Wines

In most parts of the country, spring is a time of "lightening up." We are coming out of winter and saying goodbye to those cold weather comfort foods. We change the color palates of our clothing. As we emerge from the darkness, we brighten up our foods. It's also the time to freshen up your wine identity for spring. Let's bring on the reds!

PINOT NOIR *(FRANCE)*

Pinot Noir is the world's most popular light-bodied red wine. It's loved for its red fruit, flower, and spice aromas that are accentuated by a long, smooth finish.

Made all over the world, Pinot Noir can differ in style dramatically. Originally hailing from Burgundy, the style of Pinot there is known as earthy and elegant with bright cherry fruit, yet it can have a range of delicate nuances throughout the region. On the other hand, the American Pinot Noirs from California and Oregon can be richer in fruit flavors and higher in alcohol, which makes for a fuller-flavored wine from the residual sugars of the higher alcohol content. Are you Team France or Team USA when it comes to your preference in Pinot Noir? I challenge you to start investigating your palate of these wines. Purchase bottles from Burgundy and the

U.S., blind taste them, and look for the differences. The musty notes of hay, mushroom, and lavender might delight you and find you on Team France, while the richer, fruit-driven flavors with hints of licorice and spice might sway you to Team USA. You may even branch out and find you are also a fan of the Pinot Noirs produced in New Zealand and Argentina.

Pinot Noir pairs particularly well with duck, chicken, pork, and mushrooms. I like to think of it as a catch-all, food-pairing wine—light enough for salmon but complex enough to hold up to some richer meats, including duck. In a pinch, when everyone orders a vastly different entrée at a restaurant, you can usually win by picking Pinot Noir—it will make everyone happy.

Best when served at 55°F.

GRENACHE/GARNACHA (FRANCE)

Ready to meet the second most popular grape in the world? Grenache is one of the top planted grapes in the whole world, right up there next to Cabernet Sauvignon. Grenache is in the "middle" of the red wine spectrum of acidity, tannins, and oak age. What does that really mean? It means that it is a fantastic food wine. In the Rhône Valley this indigenous grape is blended with Syrah and small amounts of other grapes to make the beautiful table wines that match French cuisine. The most famous wine made in the Rhône Valley is the *Châteauneuf-du-Pape*, which is made predominently with Grenache grapes. Translated to mean "House of the Pope," Châteauneuf-du-Pape wine was created in the 14th century for a local bishop who was elected to be pope—Pope John XXII—who also happened to be a wine lover. Grenache is the backbone of these world-famous wines.

In Spain, Grenache is known as Garnacha. Depending on where it is grown, this grape can have subtle differences. You might notice that when grown in Spain, this grape has a fruity, candy-like essence and a touch of cinnamon flavor, which complements the spiciness of the foods in Spain. It's interesting to note how the flavors of the wines reflect the style of the cuisine and terroir of each country. Wondering what the word terroir means? It's a romantic term that describes the composition of the soil, climate, topography, and overall conditions that impact the way a grape is grown.

On the island of Sardinia, Italy, they call the Grenache grape Cannonau. The difference with this grape is that it takes on more herbal notes with a touch of tannins. The Cannonau wine is a fine complement to Sardinia's rich, sheep's milk cheeses and unique Mediterranean cuisine.

Best when served at 55°F.

Sandra's Sardinia

I've been fortunate to visit Sardinia for many summers, and I've discovered that the legends are true: On Sardinia, it really is common to meet someone over 100 years old. And the culture celebrates and values its elders by placing them in a position of honor in the family. On one trip, we took a 2-hour drive from the coast to discover what it looks like to be a local. We witnessed centenarians working hard, caring for family and livestock. Natural spring water, cheese from local goats and sheep, plus their famous Cannonau wine are considered to be the secrets to their longevity. Rich in antioxidants and healthy tannins, Cannonau may just be an elixir of youth!

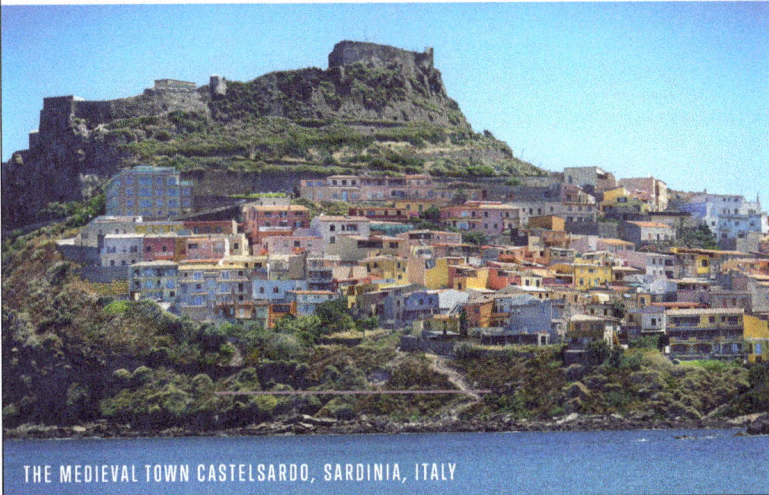

THE MEDIEVAL TOWN CASTELSARDO, SARDINIA, ITALY

CABERNET FRANC *(FRANCE)*

When Cabernet Franc fell in love with Sauvignon Blanc, the resulting love child was Cabernet Sauvignon. (Its other love child is Merlot!) This big daddy of such important wine history has generally been a blending wine of great importance, imparting complexity and herbaceous qualities to wines from the Bordeaux to Loire regions in France. But Cabernet Franc is also found as a single varietal bottled on its own.

My first experience with Cab Franc was in Solvang, California, at Buttonwood Winery. I remember this clearly because it was early in my wine education, and it stood out from everything else I was tasting and studying. To put it simply, it was as if the wine reflected the gardens and greenery with bright fruits and a wisp of herbs. Maybe it was the hazy sunset in the valley that enhanced the experience, but it was a memorable one for me, and I have enjoyed exploring Cabernet Francs ever since.

Be sure to try Cabernet Franc not only from France but also from California, Washington State, New York State, and New Zealand.

Best when served at 55°F.

Talk about deep roots. Cabernet Franc is believed to have been established in the Loire region as far back as the 17th century when a Roman Catholic cardinal had clippings of the vines brought there from southwest France. The vines were planted at the Abbey of Bourguiel; the wine is still produced in that same abbey. Cabernet Franc's origins were not officially authenticated until DNA testing in 1997.

Experiments to Try with Your Wine

Experiment #1: Wine Oxidation Challenge

My dear friend Ernie and I came up with a fun experiment to transform a cheap bottle of wine into something that tastes more expensive. We liked to buy inexpensive wines and open them on different days, being sure to mark the bottle with the dates, and then tasting them throughout the week to see how their flavor had changed. We then reported our taste findings to each other; we were always surprised to see how a wine had changed or "opened up" the longer it was exposed to air. We especially enjoyed discovering the exact amount of time it took to elevate the flavor of these affordable wines, to make them taste much more expensive. Our inside joke: "Hey I have an awesome four-day-old bottle of $10.00 Cabernet; it's perfect! . . . Come on over!"

Create Your Own Challenge:

Buy three inexpensive bottles of red, preferably Cabernet or Malbec.

- Open one bottle five days in advance, let it breathe for an hour, then cork it up.
- Open the next bottle one day in advance, let it breathe for an hour, then cork it up.
- On the day of your taste comparison, open the third bottle an hour before tasting.

Time to taste! Ready to see where your taste buds lean and notice the dramatic difference in the flavors? The first bottle to taste is the one that has been open for one hour. The second is the bottle you opened a day before, and the third you should open is the one you opened and corked five days in advance.

You will notice that the wine that has had the least exposure to air will be high in tannins (that chalky feeling on your tongue) with very bright fruit and some acidity. Then, as you taste the wine from the one-day-old bottle and move onward to the five-day-old bottle, you will see how the tannins soften, the fruit gets rounder, and the acid quiets down.

A note on refrigeration:
Keep these wines refrigerated throughout the experiment. Bring them out about 45 minutes early to achieve 57°–58°F temperature.

Experiment #2: Aerate

I truly believe that any red wine is enhanced by aeration. Sample a taste, then bust out that fancy decanter that's collecting dust, or grab any type of water pitcher. You'll want to pour the wine from a height that allows it to get air. A good indication of this is if you hear the wine "glug" as you decant and see it froth up a bit from the air. Here's a fun experiment that will make your guests laugh. Have your friends sample a taste, then pour the bottle of wine into the blender—yes, the blender!—for 2 minutes. Air is air, and however elaborately or simply you choose to incorporate it into your wine, it will enhance your experience when sipping. You'll notice a significant difference in the way it tastes just from 2 minutes on high speed!

What, Where, and Wine

Spring

The following are some suggested wines for your spring events and holidays. The whole point of this book is to help you break out of your "wine rut" and try something different. There aren't a lot of set rules, so take these ideas and serve what you enjoy when spending time with friends and family.

- Easter Brunch—Grüner Veltliner, Bellini
- Passover—Kosher Riesling, Kosher Cabernet Franc
- Spring Brunch—Prosecco, Mimosa
- Graduation celebrations—Prosecco
- Weddings—Prosecco, Sancerre, Pinot Noir
- Bridal Showers—Bubble Bar, Grenache
- Bachelorette—Bubble Bar, Cabernet Franc
- Girls' Weekend—Falanghina, Sparkling Margarita
- St Paddy's Day—Pinot Noir, Grüner Veltliner
- Kentucky Derby—Sauvignon Blanc, Prosecco

Summer

SUMMER IS ONE OF MY FAVORITE TIMES for entertaining. Whether you're spending time at the beach with your toes in the sand, in the backyard near the BBQ, or overlooking the misty mountains, summertime is a great time to share food and wine with friends and family. Summer is also a time to enjoy wines that are lighter, brighter, fresher, and best savored while wearing bathing suits and flip-flops. Your summer "Wine Identity" is such a natural progression into the season, you may not even notice the changes in your palate as they take place alongside the miraculous moment you realize you've been wearing flip-flops for a whole week.

When you are thinking about wines for summer, think about how you will be entertaining. No matter where I am, casual outdoor meals with friends are my favorite way to go. And the wine! What a difference the wine makes to match with all the amazing opportunities summer brings. From toes in the sand to backyard parties, the wines you serve should complement the foods you are serving: salads made with fresh herbs, crisp veggies, and tomatoes from your garden; fish tacos, kabobs, teriyaki chicken, and steaks on the grill. Summer is also a perfect time to experiment with seasonal wine cocktails, so be sure to check out the recipes in this section.

Summer Wine Glasses!

With so much entertaining happening outdoors, choosing the right glassware can be a challenge. There's nothing worse than having a glass smash on your terrace and potentially injure bare feet or tiny paws. Try to get the best quality acrylic glassware on the market today that is great for patio and outdoor dining. You can prevent these glasses from fogging or getting cloudy by washing them in vinegar and water (but I put mine in the dishwasher, they get cloudy, and I live with it).

Spectrum of Summer Wines

WHITES		REDS
Prosecco	Vermentino	Gamay
Cava	Pinot Grigio	Petite Sirah
Moscato	Viognier	Zinfandel
Vinho Verde	Chardonnay (Unoaked)	
Sauvignon Blanc	Rosé	
Sancerre		

White Wines

PROSECCO *(ITALY)*

Prosecco is THE fun Summer Sparkler.

With bubbles so nice, I mention it twice! Everyone loves Prosecco in both spring and summer because it is light, fresh, lower in alcohol, and low in calories (only 80 a glass!). It's also usually reasonably priced—which makes us love it even more. Prosecco has its second fermentation in large steel tanks, not in individual bottles like Champagne, which allows for the freshness of the Glera grapes and their tropical flavors to come through. The steel tanks also give Prosecco its lighter, brighter color. If you hold up a glass of Prosecco alongside a glass of Champagne, you will probably know which is which right away. Prosecco has a clear or platinum color, while Champagne has a warmer, more golden hue. The difference in flavor between the two is also apparent from the start. That steel tank gives Prosecco a brighter fruit-forward freshness, while the traditional Champagne method in which yeast is added to the individual bottles imparts a toasty taste.

Prosecco originates from the Valdobbiadene region in Veneto, Italy, and most Prosecco wines are produced in a dry, brut style. However, due to the fruity flavors of the grapes—tropical pineapple, honeydew melon, pear, and honeysuckle—it usually seems sweeter than it is.

As I mentioned in the section on spring, Prosecco pairs well with a wide range of cuisine genres and dishes. The ideology behind pairing Prosecco is to use it as a palate cleanser alongside medium-intensity foods (chicken, tofu, shrimp, and creamy cheeses). Because of its sweet aromatics and bubbles, Prosecco also pairs well with spicy curries and Southeast Asian fare.

CAVA *(SPAIN)*

Pull out your castanets, and let's go dancing in Spain! Cava is a brut sparkling wine, closer in taste to Champagne than Prosecco and usually comes with a budget-friendly price tag. This Spanish sparkler is made in the same traditional method as Champagne, using a double fermentation process that utilizes yeast to impart a beautiful toasty flavor. Macabeu (also known as Viura in Rioja) is the primary grape used in Cava production. Then comes Xarel-lo: this grape has a lemony flavor. Another grape typically used to produce Cava is Parellada, which adds acidity and zest. It's light, lemony, and refreshing, and it goes great with creamy cheeses, fresh shellfish, corn, and veggie salads.

Best when served at 46–48°F.

MOSCATO *(ITALIAN)*

If you're a fan of sweeter citrus flavor, Moscato just might be your summer wine. With a tropical, candy quality, this wine is a refreshing poolside sipper that is lower in alcohol (usually around 5.5 percent), making it an excellent choice for a hot summer day. The word "Moscato" is Italian for the Muscat family of grapes—some of the oldest grapes in the world. Many varieties grow throughout Italy and are made into both still and sparkling wines. The grapes are typically grown in the north where it is cooler at night, which results in their brightness and acidity. Moscato d'Asti is the sparkling version; it is aromatic, sweet, and bubbly. It's fruity and refreshing, and you'll also detect the aroma of honeysuckle and fresh florals. The nectar-like viscosity will coat your tongue, while the effervescence freshens your palate. The sweetness of this wine goes great with spicy foods like green and red curries, Cajun jambalaya, and Thai lettuce wraps.

Best when served at 45°F.

VINHO VERDE *(PORTUGAL)*

A regional wine blend from Portugal, Vinho Verde is offered in white, rosé, and red varieties. The most popular style is a fun, fresh white that has a wonderful, light effervescence to the wine. Like a light wine spritzer in a bottle, Vinho Verdes are lower in alcohol and most refreshing on a hot day. They are very reasonably priced and are exceptional when served with fish tacos, mango salsa, ceviche, California rolls, teriyaki bowls, edamame salad, cilantro-lime chicken, and other summer-light, sweet-sour dishes.

Best when served at 45–48°F.

SAUVIGNON BLANC *(SEEMINGLY EVERYWHERE!)*

As I mention in the section on spring wines, the name Sauvignon Blanc means "Wild White," and the wine's primary fruit flavors are lime, green apple, passion fruit, and white peach. Depending on how ripe the grapes are when the wine is made, the flavor will range from zesty lime to flowery peach. What makes Sauvignon Blanc unique from other white wines are its other herbaceous flavors like bell pepper, jalapeño, and grass. The two most popular places—New Zealand and California—where Sauvignon Blanc is grown create very different approaches to the wine. New Zealand Sauvignon Blanc is known to have a zesty grapefruit-forward flavor; California Sauvignon Blanc wines are a bit softer but still offer a classic expression of citrus and grassiness. You will become a fan of one or the other!

Best when served at 45–48°F.

SANCERRE *(FRANCE)*

People say they love Sancerre, but what exactly is Sancerre? Made of 100 percent Sauvignon Blanc grapes, Sancerre is the Loire Valley's most recognizable appellation (the region where the wine is made), and is produced in the same area as French Sauvignon Blanc. Many of the vineyards there have "white soils" that are composed of clay and limestone. The Sauvignon Blanc grapes are grown in hilly areas, where, as with the Muscat grapes, cool nights help retain the grapes' brightness and acidity. Many of the vineyards were once under water, and the salty flavor of the soil adds to the minerality of the grape. Goat farming is a longtime tradition of the region, and goat cheese pairs incredibly well with Sancerre. Just like their treasured Sauvignon Blanc grapes, the care and well-being of the local goats are paramount to the people of the region.

If you ever have a chance to visit Sancerre, the medieval town will definitely charm you. You can visit local vineyards, walk through beautiful castles, estates, and gardens, and of course, sample the wine. Tasting notes for Sancerre wine often include flavors of grass, chive, honeysuckle, lime, grapefruit, green apple, pear, honeydew, peach, flint, straw, and sweet Meyer lemon.

Best when served at 45°F.

VERMENTINO *(ITALY)*

I have a very personal connection to the Vermentino grape. I was first introduced to this lemony, salty, crisp white wine years ago on my first trip to Sardinia, Italy, with my beau, Barry. As I mentioned in the Spring section, the local population of Sardinia is known to have a very long life expectancy, which they attribute to the local food and wine. If Vermentino is going to help me live past 100, I am certainly happy about that!

The perfect wine to enjoy with the Italian sea breeze, salty cheese, and spaghetti with clams, Vermentino is predominantly grown in Sardinia but also can be found in parts of Sicily and Corsica. The rocky granite soils of Sardinia, along with the humidity and sun, develop this grape into its aromatic freshness. My summer " Wine Identity" would not be complete without enjoying this citrusy vibrant white wine, nicely chilled, on a hot day at the beach with Barry. I encourage you to go out of your comfort zone and give this delicious wine a try.

Best when served at 45°F.

PINOT GRIGIO *(ITALY)*

I will admit here that my personal "Wine Identity" rut that I get stuck in, out of convenience and habit, is to order a Pinot Grigio at almost any restaurant I go to. Why is that?

Not just for summer, Pinot Grigio is a fabulous go-to, year-round white wine, that ticks all the boxes of many wine lovers. Its fruity roundness and touch of citrus make it a perfect complement to most foods, particularly during the summer. It enhances flavors of fresh herbs and grilled fish with faint honeyed notes and floral aromas like honeysuckle, while with its twinkle of acidity, it's an especially perfect match for fresh tomatoes still warm from the sun, picked from your garden.

Pinot Grigio made its splashy debut in America back in the 1970s. It was an instant hit and achieved immediate celebrity status—the vineyards in Italy actually went into overdrive to fulfill the thirst of America. This resulted in a lot of mass-produced Pinot Grigio that was vastly varied in taste and quality, which ranged from good to not so good.

The best Pinot Grigios primarily hail from northern Italy in an area called Alto Adige, a picturesque region renowned for its verdant valleys. The varietal—known for its grayish-blue color when ripe—also thrives in the cooler climates of Austria, Hungary, Slovenia, parts of Germany (known in German as Ruländer or Grauburgunder), France, and even Turkey. Oh, and of course, there are great Pinot Grigios in California, too! No wonder Pinot Grigio is so popular—this thirst-quenching, friendly wine sure gets around.

Best when served at 45–48°F.

Asian Tuna Platter

Here is a recipe of mine that is a perfect entrée for any summer occasion. Make it in advance; serve it at room temperature. What could be easier? Be sure to wait to drizzle the dressing until just before serving.

Ingredients

- 2 lbs. fresh tuna steaks
- 2 Tbsp. Chinese five-spice powder
- 1 whole papaya, seeded and sliced into inch-thick slices

- 1 lb. fresh mozzarella ball
- 2 large garden tomatoes sliced not too thin
- 1 bag of bean sprouts
- ½ cup chopped cilantro
- ½ cup chopped scallions
- ¼ cup toasted almond slices
- sesame seeds
- olive oil (for searing tuna)

Dressing

This dressing recipe is very flexible. I often don't measure when I make it, so feel free to make it sweeter or spicier to suit your tastes.

- 2 Tbsp. soy sauce
- 2 Tbsp. rice wine vinegar
- 2 Tbsp. honey
- 1 Tbsp. fresh orange juice
- 2 Tbsp. sesame oil
- 1 tsp. balsamic vinegar

Directions

Pat tuna steaks all over with Chinese five-spice powder and sesame seeds. Pan sear on medium to high in olive oil, 2–3 minutes a side till desired rareness (I like it very rare!). Set aside.

To Assemble

- Place bean sprouts on platter.
- Slice tuna steaks into inch-and-a-half-thick slices.
- Layer the tuna, papaya, tomato, and mozzarella on top of sprouts.
- Sprinkle cilantro, toasted almond slices, and chopped scallions on top.
- *If making ahead of time, save the dressing until right before serving.* Drizzle about half of the dressing on top; have the rest available to add if your guests want more.
- Serve at room temperature.

Serve with a chilled Pinot Grigio, Rosé, or if you are feeling racy, try a chilled Gamay!

VIOGNIER *(FRANCE)*

The Viognier grape makes a full-bodied white wine that originally hails from the South of France. When you smell this wine, you will notice fresh tropical flavors with a delightful hint of white flowers waiting to be savored. It can be a heady surprise if you're not familiar with this varietal, which is now being produced in many other parts of the world as well. If you are a Chardonnay fan, Viognier will absolutely enchant you with its body and depth, and it will delight your senses.

The medium acidity and ripe fruit makes it a perfect accompaniment to a summer cheese board. Also, you can enjoy it along with shellfish, lighter herb and butter cuisine, nuts and sesame seeds, and dried tropical fruits. This is one of my favorite white wines because it reminds me of the vibrant, verdant herbs and bounty of fragrant flowers in my summer garden.

Best when served at 45–48°F.

CHARDONNAY (UNOAKED) *(FRANCE)*

One of my personal favorites is Chardonnay from France. I find that these wines are so much more food-friendly and flexible than the big, oaky California Chards. Those Cali Chards have an amazing cult following, and I get it! But the rich butter, peach, and oak can squash a light summer meal. Chardonnay from the Burgundy/Borgogne region is crisp with green apple, lemon, and a touch of mineral saltiness. The grapes are fermented in steel, which allows the complex fruit and mineral essence to shine in each bottle.

Burgundy is a beautiful area of France that has many wine "neighborhoods" (also known as "appellations") where exceptional wines are produced. But the two major areas that have the most accessible wines in our wine shops in the U.S. are Chablis and Mâconnais.

The area of Chablis is about 80 miles northwest of Dijon. The Chardonnay there is traditionally fermented in stainless steel, concrete, or neutral oak. Chablis popularized this style, and soon everyone around the world started labeling their unoaked Chardonnays with the word "Chablis" until France complained. Unoaked Chardonnay tastes only of the varietal characteristics of Chardonnay, which are green apple, lemon, and sometimes pineapple with a long, tingly finish.

Mâconnais is the southern part of Burgundy where the weather is a bit warmer and the Chardonnay grapes provide a bigger and more fruit-forward flavor with touches of tropical notes. You might even find some of the more expensive Mâconnais Chardonnay with a touch of oak, which would make you California Chardonnay lovers happy.

How to tell the difference between Chablis and Mâconnais? Chablis white wine is going to have a fresh elegance of apple, melon, and light acidity that dances on your tongue; it is well paired with sole meunière, goat cheese tarts, shellfish, and pork with mushrooms. Mâconnais Chardonnay wine is a fuller fruit wine where you'll notice the warmer tropical notes; it can be paired with smoked salmon, risotto, roast chicken with vegetables, and meaty fish (such as sea bass, swordfish, tuna).

Serving Chardonnay

Serve unoaked Chardonnays closer to 50°F. The serving temperature of an unoaked Chardonnay should be different than an oaked one and here is why: if you serve the oaky Chardonnays too cold it will mask the buttery oaky flavors this wine is known to impart.

What's at Your Summer Farmers' Market?

Our local farmers' market has the most fantastic choices in the summer. The bright colors and collections of fresh produce are so beautiful I feel like every farm stand is a work of art worthy of a watercolor. Make sure you take the time to visit your local farmers' market, grab a fresh baguette, and whatever "looks good." If you're wondering what wines to pair with which fresh foods, here are a few thought starters:

- Bring out the taste of local carrots, beets, and hearty greens with Sancerre.
- Fresh scallops from the fishmonger go great with Vermentino.
- Omelets made with local eggs and veggies pair perfectly with Chablis.

Summer entertaining should never be stressful. To make a simple moment into a memorable occasion, go with the flow, and look to your local farmers' market for inspiration!

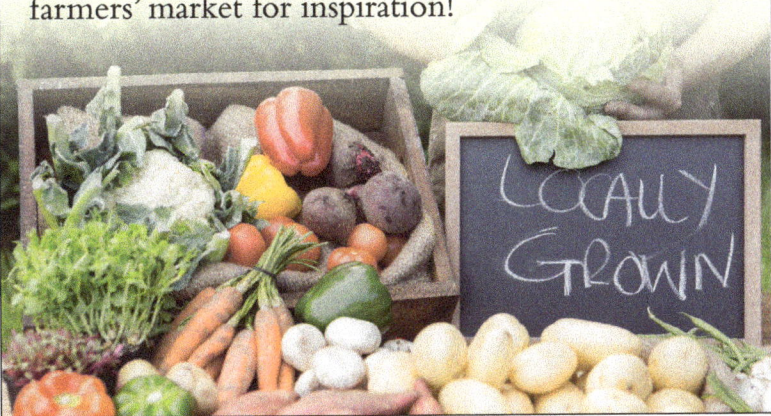

ROSÉ *(VARIOUS LOCATIONS)*

"Oh it's pink? I don't like sweet wine," is a common reaction when I have served Rosé. People often think that all pink wine is sweet White Zinfandel, which was actually a "mistake" made by a winemaker in California in the 1970s. This accidental blend of barrels created the infamous sweet pink wine that overtook America from the 1970s through the 1990s. So, in early 2000, when French Rosé started to become fashionable, people did not embrace it immediately. Unbeknownst to these skeptical folks who had one too many college hangovers from the sweet pink stuff, these Rosé wines are bone dry and full of acidity and wisps of berry, which makes this wine crisp, food-friendly, and perfect for summertime.

This wine is no mistake. In fact, it has become an important staple of summer wines. It is made in the old traditional way of letting the skins of the grapes kiss the wine just long enough to impart a perfect pinkness and light berry flavor. Rosés are made from many different grapes depending on their country of origin: the most famous are from Provence, France, where Grenache, Syrah, and Mourvèdre are used. In Italy, the wines can be made from Nebbiolo; in Spain, they use Garnacha and Tempranillo.

Each one of these Rosés will have a distinct style from the other—some will be darker in color and richer in berry flavor. I personally love Rosés from Provence, which often have a light flavor of watermelon candy with a touch of lemon. No matter which one you prefer,

Rosés are a perfect complement to summer food fare such as fresh tomatoes from the garden, shrimp salads, oysters, and white fish tacos.

Best when served at 40°–45°F.

Watermelon Frosé

My favorite refreshing summer aperitif is Watermelon Frosé. It is very simple to make:

In a blender, mix a cup of ice, a cup of diced watermelon fruit, and two cups of Rosé. The magic ingredient that puts this over the top is a handful of fresh basil—add that to the blender, too. Serve with straws and sip in the shade.

Another option is to use fresh strawberries and/or raspberries with fresh mint. Delightful!

Red Wines

GAMAY *(FRANCE)*

Hooray, hooray for Gamay! This is the little black dress of summer reds—just pluck it from your wine rack, and you can be sure it will go with nearly any summer cuisine. Always fruity and floral, and sometimes an earthy, light-bodied red, Gamay is the main grape varietal that produces this delectable wine that's similar to Pinot Noir, but juicier! Planted in the region of Beaujolais, France—a historic province, just north of Lyon—Gamay is actually called a "cousin of Pinot Noir," which is grown in Burgundy, a neighbor of Beaujolais.

Loved for its delicate floral aromas, subtle earthy notes, and surprising ability to pair with food—especially grilled tuna and salmon—Gamay features a welcome nose reminiscent of a bouquet of fresh-cut violets, iris, and peony flowers wrapped in cherry, raspberry, and plum with subtle spice. Be sure to serve this fruity beauty nicely chilled.

Best when served at 45–48°F.

Big, Bad BBQ Wines

Pick from this selection of remarkable Reds that are sure to label your BBQ a resounding success!

FOR YOUR *SAVORY* BBQ:
Petite Sirah

This wine has an interesting past, and it just may have a bright future ahead. Petite Sirah was very popular in the U.S. and served at the dinner tables of all the best families in the Victorian Era. Yet somehow it fell out of favor as other grapes were introduced in California. It is not one of the most popular wines, but I think it should be. It's reasonably priced, lush in flavor, and very yummy. I have shown this wine at many corporate events, and my guests have always been delighted by its full-bodied flavors of blueberry, chocolate, and black pepper.

The Petite Sirah Identity Crisis

Make no mistake about it; Petite Sirah is not a smaller version of Syrah; it's a distinct grape variety. Petite Sirah is the offspring of Syrah and Peloursin. If you've never heard of Peloursin, that's understandable; it's a very rare, red French wine grape.

With its smoky fruit flavors, Petite Sirah will pair nicely with bold exotic spices and herbs—just avoid overly sweet recipes such as sugary barbecue sauce. It is better paired with grilled meats and more savory foods such as thick portobello mushrooms and herby Chimichurris that add brightness to your meatier fishes, cauliflower steaks, savory steaks, and other carnivore delights.

Best when served at 55–60°F

FOR YOUR *SWEET* BBQ:
Zinfandel

Zinfandel wine is a bold, fruit-forward red that's loved for its jammy fruit and smoky, exotic spice notes.

The primary flavors of Zinfandel are jam, blueberry, black pepper, cherry, plum, boysenberry, cranberry, and licorice. When you taste Zinfandel it often explodes in your mouth with candied fruitiness followed by spice and often a warm, tobacco-like finish.

The hearty, bold flavors in Zinfandel make it a natural companion for the rich and flavorful world of BBQ. Try ribs, grilled chicken, roast lamb, pulled pork, pork chops—all enjoyed with your various sweet and tangy BBQ sauces. Try it with a peach or bourbon glaze, teriyaki, molasses, or steakhouse sauces.

Best when served at 60°–65°F.

California Cowboy BBQ

One story I love to share is about my friends Missy and Hank from Ojai, California. Hank grew up in Santa Maria and is from an old California bull-riding family that was also known for their BBQ. His mother, Mary, would make these fantastic homemade tortillas, and they would roast tri-tip steaks that were marinated in red wine, garlic, and rosemary. To this day, the smell of roasted steaks can transport me to that extraordinary place, sitting out under the stars in that orchard, listening to his family laugh and share stories of a life very different from my own. The tradition of marinating and grilling tri-tip (also known as triangle steak) is first known to have occurred in Santa Maria, California, during the 1950s.

Choose a bold, flavorful Zinfandel to serve with this delicious recipe. It's smoky, jammy, and just perfect with this flavorful yet lower cost cut of beef. You can use this same marinade with T-bones or filet mignon as well, but I promise you, there's nothing quite like this authentic cowboy-style meal.

What you need
- 2- to 3-pound tri-tip steak
- ½ cup hearty red wine, such as Cabernet or Sangiovese
- 4 cloves garlic, finely minced
- 2 Tbsp. fresh rosemary leaves
- ¼ cup olive oil

Directions
- Put the tri-tip steak in a bowl or bag with the marinade of red wine, garlic, rosemary leaves, and olive oil.
- Refrigerate for 4–6 hours, turning frequently. Can marinate overnight.
- Remove the steak from the refrigerator; discard the marinade.
- On a hot grill, grill for about 10–12 minutes on each side for medium-rare steak.
- Let the steak rest for a few minutes for the best flavor, and then slice it into very thin slices at an angle across the grain.

What, Where, and Wine

Summer

- Backyard BBQ—Zinfandel
- Fourth of July fireworks (red, white, and sparkles)—American Cabernet and Chardonnay, also Prosecco
- Summer sunset sipper—Viognier
- Flip-flops and beach sand—Vinho Verde, Cava
- Wines for the boat—Rosé
- Clambakes/lobsters—Chardonnay
- Oyster shucking—Sauvignon Blanc, Sancerre
- Rooftop soirée—Aperol Spritz
- Summer S'mores—Zinfandel
- Picnic in the park—Gamay
- Pool party—Sauvignon Blanc, Vinho Verde
- Polo matches—Rosé

Warm Weather Cheese Board
It's Summer . . . Say Cheese!

How could I write a book about wine without the perfect accompaniment—cheese? My friend Erin Hedley of La Dame du Fromage helped me put together some great tips that make creating a warm weather cheese board to accompany some fantastic summer wine. As Erin says: "Cheese boards have the power to bring people together at any gathering—to linger, ooh, ahh, taste, explore, and learn about the cheeses, their locales, and legends."

Ingredients in Photo

- Coupole (goat cheese)
- Ossau-Iraty (sheep's milk cheese)
- Taleggio (cow's milk)
- Fresh summer fruits and berries
- Dried apricots and candied orange slices
- Almonds and cashews
- Edible apple blossoms or nasturtium

Erin's Tips

Make sure you get a selection of cheeses made with different milks from goats, cows, and sheep. They will have contrasting flavors of tart, salty, and sweet. They are best at room temperature, so take the cheeses out from refrigeration an hour before you serve them.

Colors of the Cheeses

- Goat cheese: milky white
- Sheep: ivory
- Cow: yellow

Summery condiments to complement the three styles of cheese are lemon marmalade, honey, and strawberry compote.

For crackers: Choose olive oil and sea salt or rice crackers; these crackers won't overpower the cheese.

Experiment with color! Fruits, fresh herbs, greens, edible summer flowers, and even cut vegetables will all add a beautiful pop to your platters.

THE CHEESE THAT CHANGED MY LIFE:
Coupole Goat Cheese from France

Coupole is a spectacular cheese that changed my perspective about what goat cheese is all about. With its wrinkly rind, creamy layer, and rich, almost fudge-like center, this goat cheese provides you with a unique experience. It has a creamy, lemony essence that is beautiful when paired with a sparkling wine or a Sancerre. Serving bubbles with creamy cheese is a perfect pairing because the refreshing bubbles cleanse your palate between each creamy bite.

Erin of La Dame du Fromage says, "If you can't find Coupole, seek out Crottin de Chavignol or other French goat cheeses. My best advice is to find an artisan goat cheese with a nice, wrinkly rind and save the fresh, crumbly goat cheeses for salads."

Fall

SOME PEOPLE FEEL MELANCHOLY at the end of summer, but not me. Maybe it's my poetic New England soul, but fall is a time for beginnings to me. It will always feel like a new school year has started, though instead of a new lunch box, I get a new purse.

During apple-picking season, we are inspired to bake apple crisps, add fresh apples to cook alongside our roasts, and prepare our favorite family meals. Everywhere in the country it's time for festive tailgates, Halloween parties, and that oh-so-important Thanksgiving dinner. So what will your Wine Identity be this fall? It's time to move from the refreshing light wines of summer into the richer, fuller, cooler weather wines that match fall cuisine and events. Read on to learn about some delicious wines and discover some of my personal favorite fall recipes.

Spectrum of Fall Wines

WHITES	REDS
Fumé Blanc	Merlot
Cortese/Gavi	Tempranillo
Torrontés	Monastrell/Mourvèdre
Chablis	Nero d'Avola
	Syrah/Shiraz

White Wines

FUMÉ BLANC/POUILLY-FUMÉ *(FRANCE)*

This is an excellent white wine for Sauvignon Blanc fans to savor in the fall. Pouilly-Fumé is Sauvignon Blanc from the Loire region of France that is aged in oak barrels. The first thing you notice when you pour it in your glass is the wisp of smoke from the oak aging. From the nose, you could almost be tricked that this is a light Chardonnay. The signature is when you finish the sip, you experience the clean taste of citrus.

The nickname "Fumé Blanc" was conceived in California when it was decided to age the wine in oak barrels instead of steel tanks. Sauvignon Blanc is aged in steel tanks, while Fumé Blanc is Sauvignon Blanc aged in oak barrels.

The saying, "You are what you eat," applies to grapes, too. This grape is known for offering a spectrum of aromatic qualities and flavors that vary based on where it is grown and how the wine is aged. The soils influence the flavor profile and aromatic personality. Sauvignon Blanc grows well in sand, chalk, gravel, or smoky gunflint. Sandy soils bring out the herbaceous flavors; clay gives more fruit and body, while chalk adds more minerality. Fumé Blanc can be enjoyed with richer, creamier cheeses and foods, as the slight oak in this wine adds to its body.

This wine-making style imparts the slight woodsy flavor, while retaining some crisp acidity. For Sauvignon Blanc fans, the whisper of smoke provides a fuller flavor, offering a nice transition for the cooler weather. I like to serve Fumé Blanc with smoked salmon, grilled vegetables, and roast chicken with creamy mustard sauce.

Best when served at 48°–50°F.

CORTESE/GAVI *(ITALY)*

Gavi is a fuller bodied white wine than Fumé Blanc, with a surprising herbaceous bite that will usher summer wine fans into the fall.

I have wonderful memories of tasting this wine on my first trip to Milan, Italy, as a young woman. During one of my first evening meals out with a group of my fellow Americans and a few Italian locals, I was introduced to Gavi white wine. I later learned that this wine is one of the most popular dinner wines in Italy. It has a bright floral and peach flavor with fresh aromatics for the nose and a light spice essence that tastes spicier and more sumptuous than a summery Sauvignon Blanc. You may even notice a touch of almond. It has a greenish-yellow color in your glass, which reflects the lime flavor and oak aging.

Crafted in the Piedmont region of northwest Italy with the grape named Cortese, the vines of the Cortese grape need a consistent "hands-on" approach in their care—or they falter. In fact, you could think of this wine as a bit of a diva! With its enticing, ripe melon flavor, Gavi pairs beautifully with spiced chicken dishes like tandoori, and also any recipes that feature cured ham, smoked cheeses, and chicken scarpariello.

Best when served at 48°–50°F.

Gavi:
A Pre-Roman Town Worth Exploring!

In the town of Gavi, the Cortese grape dates back to the 1600s. Vineyards that grow this special varietal surround the rolling hills of the town, which is topped by a pre-Roman era castle. In the Middle Ages, the castle walls were reconstructed, turning the castle into a fortress that can be explored today. Historic festivals are held in August each year and feature locals dressed in period costumes while they celebrate the wonderful Gavi wine. *Salute!*

TORRONTÉS *(ARGENTINA)*

Torrontés is similar to other aromatic white wines, including Riesling and Muscat Blanc (Moscato). The major difference is that Torrontés is commonly made in a dry style. This creates a very interesting wine to enjoy because its salty lean taste is in opposition to its sweet perfumed aromas. Albariño and dry styles of Riesling and Muscat Blanc (dry "Moscatel" is mostly found in Portugal) are similar in aroma and taste to Torrontés.

In spite of its sweet aroma, Torrontés is usually quite dry, making it a great match with savory dishes that feature exotic spices, fruit, and aromatic herbs.

Best when served at 48°–50°F.

CHABLIS *(FRANCE)*

For some, the word "Chablis" evokes images of big green jugs of wine in the late 1970s. A memory of my mom and our next-door neighbor sitting on the front stairs sipping from a glass filled with the yellowish liquid is ingrained in my mind. But this doesn't do justice to what a beautiful wine Chablis is! Chablis is a classic, elegant white wine from the Chablis region—where Chardonnay is also produced in Burgundy, France—that sometimes gets a bad rap. It's a dinner wine that will not let you down. I have presented Chablis at many of my corporate events to a delightful response. Don't let its old reputation mislead you; this is a dependable, crowd-pleaser that possesses flavors of citrus and pear with a crisp, fresh finish of minerality (thanks to the mineral-rich clay in the Chablis area soil) and makes for an elegant, food-friendly dinner wine. Aged less in barrels, Chablis does not have the heavy oak, buttery flavor of California Chards, and should absolutely be on your go-to list for wines this fall.

Best when served at 55°–58°F.

Though one might think the capital of the Burgundy region would be related to wine, it's not! The capital is actually Dijon . . . and guess what the city's known for? Dijon is also home to the fabulous Musée des Beaux-Arts (est. 1787) and the grand Palace of the Dukes of Burgundy where construction began in 1364. Back then, they did not yet have mustard in Dijon, but by the 1500s they had Chablis—and a few centuries later (late 1880s), we had California Chardonnay!

Pumpkin Hummus Served in a Pumpkin!

Fall is a favorite time to sit around the fire pit with friends and enjoy the colors of the season and the cool air. I love to make this simple and healthy hummus in my food processor. It picks up the favorite flavors of the season and goes great with a variety of wines.

Pro tip:
Make Pumpkin Hummus the day before and let the flavors intensify before serving. If you can find a small sugar pumpkin at the grocery store or Farmers' Market, turn it into a cute serving bowl when you scoop it out and fill it with this hummus!

Pumpkin Hummus

Ingredients

- 2 Tbsp. lemon juice
- 2 Tbsp. tahini
- 3 cloves garlic
- ¾ tsp. salt
- 2 (15 oz.) cans garbanzo beans, drained
- 2 tsp. extra-virgin olive oil
- 1 (15 oz.) can pumpkin puree
- 1 tsp. ground cumin
- 1 tsp. curry powder (or to taste)
- ½ tsp. cayenne pepper
- ¼ cup toasted pumpkin seed kernels, or more to taste
- 1 pinch paprika

Directions

- **Step 1**—Hollow out a small sugar pumpkin. (You can reserve the seeds to toast by spreading them on a cookie sheet, sprinkling with salt, and roasting them at 375°F for up to 20 minutes or until golden brown. Or you can purchase toasted seeds.)
- **Step 2**—Pulse lemon juice, tahini, garlic, and salt together in a food processor or blender until

smooth. Add garbanzo beans and olive oil and pulse until smooth. Add pumpkin, cumin, curry, and cayenne pepper; process until well blended. Transfer hummus to a container with a lid and refrigerate at least 2 hours.

- **Step 3**—Slice the pumpkin shell horizontally in half (like a bowl), and then transfer the hummus into the bottom shell.
- **Step 4**—Before serving, garnish with paprika and a sprinkling of toasted pumpkin seeds.

Pumpkin Spice Season Is Here
– Mull It Over! –

We just can't get enough! Once the leaves start to change, the pumpkin spice appears. You'll find it in lattes, tortilla chips, muffins, and even as a special ingredient in body scrubs. Now you can expand your wine identity into pumpkin spice as well. I've got the perfect warm mulled wine to share at your football tailgate party, sip après leaf peeping with friends, and bring as a special treat for your fall book group. My friends Deb and Tom have an amazing Party Barn. I brought the following fabulous creation to their fall gathering—it was a huge hit.

Pumpkin Spice Mulled Wine

Ingredients

- 2 bottles of medium-bodied dry red wine (Côtes du Rhône, Pinot Noir)
- 1 cup brown sugar
- ¼ cup honey
- 4 Tbsp. pumpkin pie spice (a little more if you really love it!)
- 1 cinnamon stick
- Sliced clementines (keep the peel on)
- Optional: add cloves to taste

Directions

Combine all ingredients. Put in a slow cooker on low and let it mull for 1–2 hours.

Red Wines

MERLOT *(FRANCE)*

Merlot is a smooth, food-friendly wine that is dry and fruity. As the elegant dark garnet color swirls in your goblet, you'll notice it's a perfect shade to match your latest fall nail polish. This grape is the mellow stepbrother to the bigger personality of Cabernet Sauvignon. Both Cabernet and Merlot are considered the most popular red wines in the world. They derive from the Cabernet Franc grape; the difference between them is that the Cabernet grape offers up more acidity and robustness, while Merlot has a more velvety softness. If you have Merlot on your mind, it means you're wishing for supple and soft tannins with rich black cherry and a hint of chocolate. It almost sounds like a luscious piece of chocolate cake! It's a perfect cool weather red wine to sip by your outdoor fire pit, while enjoying some charcuterie or chocolate.

Best when served at 55–58°F.

Fruity Wine? It's Divine!

Guess what? You might not realize it, but you probably like "fruity" red wine. A common "Wine Identity" is when you hear a wine described as fruity, you assume it's very sweet and not dry. Many times when I mention that a particular wine is fruity, a client will say, "Oh, but I don't like sweet wines." However, when a wine is described as fruity, it simply means that while the predominant, noticeable flavors are from the lush red ripe fruit in the wine, the flavor profile is supported by oak, vanilla, herbs, lavender, clove, and chocolate. This creates a balanced wine such as Cabernet Sauvignon, Syrah/Shiraz, Merlot, Rioja, and Zinfandel.

TEMPRANILLO *(SPAIN)*

When you're craving something different in a red wine, something savory, Tempranillo—Spain's #1 wine grape— is the answer. With the bold structure of Cabernet Sauvignon and the meaty heartiness of Carignan, Tempranillo features dominant, memorable flavors of cherry, dried fig, cedar, tobacco, and dill. Yummy, right? When it's young, it can be surprisingly fresh and fruity; with oak and age, it yields to the dusty, tobacco, and leather flavors that serious wine lovers crave.

Made famous by Rioja, where wines are, in part, classified by how long they age in oak, a well-made Tempranillo is aged for twenty years. That's two decades. Wow. The result is remarkable, and pairs nicely with steak, gourmet burgers, and rack of lamb. Fresher styles match well with baked pasta and other tomato-based dishes. And though popular to serve with red meat and ham, Tempranillo is a surprisingly versatile food wine that can be quite pleasing with roasted vegetables, hearty pastas, smoky, starchy entrées, and even Mexican food.

Best when served at 55°–58°F.

MONASTRELL *(SPAIN)* / MOURVÈDRE *(FRANCE)*

This one big bold grape is known by two names. In Spain it is known as Monastrell and is made into a rough and chewy red wine with hints of dried cherry and tobacco. Monastrell wines have been the highlight of central Spain for thousands of years.

In Rhône, France, this grape is called Mourvèdre, and is often blended with other grapes. It creates a backbone of strength in wines throughout the Rhône Valley. With hints of raisin and a touch of smoky oak, this is a heady wine that fills your senses.

Try them both: they will pair amazingly well with big fall recipes of lamb, red meat, and rich pasta dishes with red sauce.

Best when served at 55°–58°F.

NERO d'AVOLA *(SICILY)*

The name might sound like it belongs to the leading man in a romance novel, but it's actually the name of a terribly sexy grape. Though this might not seem like a familiar varietal, you will find this delicious, rich red wine readily available in your local wine shops. As one of the most important wines from the island of Sicily, Italy, Nero d'Avola creates a full and fruity wine with flavors of dark cherry and hints of tobacco that will make any Cabernet lover happy.

Highly respected and widely planted, Nero d'Avola literally has had its roots in Sicily since at least the Middle Ages, when the rich, purple-red grapes were often blended with lesser wines to add color and body. Today, Nero d'Avola—translation: *Black of Avola*—is also grown in California, Australia, Malta, Turkey, and South Africa. With a balance of rich tannins and lush fruit, it's a perfect red wine to be enjoyed with a great pepperoni pizza and even with bowls of spicy chili, and it is a terrific, approachable wine to keep in stock for Wednesday night pasta and meatballs!

Best when served at 55°–58°F.

HALLOWEEN WINE CHALLENGE:
Which Wine Goes Best with the Candy You Steal from Your Kids?

- **Prosecco**—Lemon Sour Patch Kids or Starbursts, Smarties, Sweet Tarts, Almond Joy
- **Sauvignon Blanc**—Lime or Lemon Sour Patch Kids
- **Chardonnay**—Butterfingers, Almond Joy, Kit Kat, Twix, dried apricots
- **Pinot Noir**—Reese's Peanut Butter Cups, Kit Kat, Hershey's Milk Chocolate Bar, Twix, M&M's, dried cherries
- **Cabernet Sauvignon**—Snickers, Reese's Peanut Butter Cups, Twix

SYRAH *(FRANCE) (AMERICA)*
SHIRAZ *(AUSTRALIA)*

As I mentioned before, wines can take up different flavors based on the terroir, culture, and the winemaking style of the regions where they are produced. Syrah grapes are grown all over the world, and they create many delicious wines for you to try. I encourage you to explore the Syrahs I feature here first to discover which style Syrah you "identify" with the most.

- **French Syrah:** With full fruit and light and bright tannins, this makes an elegant and refined table wine. The limestone and clay soil impart a mineral freshness into the Syrah grape. Grown predominantly in the Rhône Valley, it is blended into the classic Côtes du Rhône wines, the red blend from this area.

- **American Syrah:** In America, we tend to go big, and our red wines are no exception. Typically higher in alcohol content, American Syrah grapes are grown in farmland soil that's enriched with loam, clay, and sand. You can count on these wines to show up with big jammy blackberry and cocoa flavors.

- **Australian Shiraz:** Different spelling, same grape. These wines are as rugged as the valleys in which they are grown. The dry sand and clay, along with the hotter climate, bring out the bold spice and wild fruit flavors of this wine. This grape has nice tannins that complement the richer foods we enjoy in the fall, including spicy chili, grilled steak, and cool-weather charcuterie boards.

Best when served at 55°–60°F.

THANKSGIVING

Thanksgiving dinner can be the most complicated of meals. Not only do you have to plan an elaborate menu, but you also need to entertain a mix of personalities that includes cousins, in-laws, siblings—and sometimes added friends! You'd better have some great wines on hand to get through it. The many regions and multicultural influences across the country inspire our Thanksgiving menus. From New England traditions to those of the spicy Southwest, I've selected some great American wines to pair with your favorite holiday meal of the year. It's a great time to celebrate American wines on this all-American holiday! Here are a few suggestions for wine pairings.

Southern Menu

Food: Turkey or ham, sweet potato casserole with marshmallows, sausage gravy and biscuits, cheese grits, mac and cheese, cornbread stuffing.

Wine: A dry Riesling with flavors of citrus and pear along with a mineral crispness is a perfect match for dishes of the south—from the sweet to the creamy.

Southwest Menu

Food: Chili-rubbed roast turkey, chorizo sausage stuffing, corn tamales, and chili-spiced mashed sweet potatoes.

Wine: All these warm spices deserve a rich, full fruit wine. Syrah is a lush wine with dark fruit and spice that will beautifully handle your warm spicy dinner.

New England Menu

Food: Oyster stuffing, Parker House rolls, roasted butternut squash with apples, and cranberry sauce. For a multicultural experience, try lasagna or manicotti; for traditional fare, serve roast turkey, creamed onions, mashed potatoes, and stuffing. (My old Yankee family hardly ever had anything green, except maybe peas, though we definitely NEVER once had green salad on Thanksgiving.)

Wines: California Chardonnay and all its round, buttery flavor is a favorite across New England. The tropical fruit notes and the buttery essence complement your roast turkey. All the big personalities around your dinner table deserve a big red wine! California Cabernet Sauvignon is a bold and robust Cab to stand up to Nonna's lasagna . . . as well as Grandma's favorite stuffing.

Midwest Menu

Food: Cheesy broccoli casserole, roast turkey, wild rice, mashed potatoes with bacon, green bean casserole with crispy onions, cheese balls, and deviled eggs.

Wine: With a bright cranberry and plum flavor that has hints of chocolate, Pinot Noir from the Willamette Valley in Oregon is perfectly suited to complement cheeses, roasted veggies, and other midwestern dishes.

My Personal Stuffing Challenge

When I was a child in New Hampshire, my grandfather "Dave" was in charge of the Thanksgiving stuffing every year. He would get quite creative with chestnuts, beer, cornbread, and even oysters. (New England was an oyster mecca in the 1800s, and many old recipes include them.) We all remember the year Gramps made the oyster stuffing! He never followed exact recipes but instead used his great sense of taste and whimsy to create delicious stuffing while sipping his "Whoopdidoo" cocktail and singing songs by Dean Martin. Now that I am grown and have a family of my own, I attempt to recreate this, one of his greatest stuffing masterpieces, and serve it with a Chablis.

Grandpa Dave's Oyster Stuffing

Ingredients

- 2 loaves Italian or French bread (1 lb. total), cut into small cubes (12 cups)
- ½ lb. sliced bacon, cut into ½ inch pieces
- 2 to 3 Tbsp. butter
- 2 medium onions, finely chopped (2 cups)
- 1 cup chopped celery
- 3 Tbsp. chopped fresh thyme
- 1 Tbsp. finely chopped fresh sage
- 1 Tbsp. finely chopped garlic
- ½ tsp. salt

- ground black pepper
- ⅔ cup finely chopped fresh flat-leaf parsley
- 18 oysters, shucked, drained, and chopped (¾ cup)
- 2½ cups chicken broth

Directions

Preheat your oven to 325°F.

Spread bread cubes in two shallow baking pans and bake in upper and lower thirds of the oven, switching the position of the pans halfway through baking, until golden, 25–30 minutes total. Cool bread in pans on racks, then transfer to a large bowl.

Meanwhile, cook bacon in a 12-inch heavy skillet over moderate heat, stirring occasionally, until crisp, about 10 minutes. Transfer to paper towels to drain and reserve the fat in the skillet.

If bacon renders less than ¼ cup fat, add enough oil to total ¼ cup fat. Cook onions, celery, thyme, sage, garlic, salt, and pepper in fat in a skillet over moderate heat, stirring occasionally, for 8–10 minutes, until vegetables are softened. Transfer to a bowl with bread cubes, then stir in bacon, parsley, butter, and oysters. Drizzle with chicken broth, then season with salt and pepper and toss well.

Transfer stuffing to a buttered 3–3½-quart shallow baking dish. Bake, covered, in the middle of the oven for 30 minutes; uncover and bake until browned, about 30 minutes more. Grandpa and I fill the cavity of the bird with oyster stuffing, but I leave that decision up to you.

What, Where, and Wine

Fall

- Football tailgate—Shiraz, Gavi
- Apple picking—Nebbiolo, Chablis
- Pumpkin spice season—Syrah, Grüner Veltliner, Merlot
- Winery visit with the girls/Harvest fun— Grenache, Chablis
- Halloween candy and wine pairings—Nero d'Avola or Merlot with Reese's Peanut Butter Cups! Grüner Veltliner and Sour Patch candies
- Fire pit, S'mores, and wine—Merlot (the cherry and chocolate in this wine will complement the chocolate and marshmallow), Chablis
- Thanksgiving—Merlot or Syrah (depending on the spice level of your family recipes). Cortese (Gavi) will be a good white to hold up to this varied meal
- Leaf peeping/Autumn train tours—Tempranillo, Chablis, Monastrell
- Slow Cooker meals—Monastrell, Grenache, Chablis, the fuller bodied white will hold up nicely to your dinner

Cool Weather Cheese Board

Erin Hedley of La Dame du Fromage shares the following amazing tips for a cool weather cheese board, which is significantly different from the cheeses of a warm weather board. While the warm weather board is focused on accenting the lightness of the season, the cool weather board showcases the more rustic and hearty cheeses that complement cooler temperatures so nicely. And though some of the cheese listed here might stretch your budget, the main point is to not have all the cheeses from one source; instead, offer a variety of cow, goat, and sheep's milk cheeses. Also, be sure to include a variety of textures and flavors.

Ingredients

- River's Edge Chèvre (goat cheese)
- 15-month Comté (French cow's milk cheese)
- Moliterno al Tartufo (Italian sheep's milk cheese with truffle)
- Aged Gouda (Reypenaer)
- Delice de Bourgogne
- Vacherin Mont d'Or (only available in the winter)
- Stilton blue cheese
- Tuscan salami (roll and twist the slices to create "salami rivers")
- Fresh figs, persimmons, starfruit, strawberries
- Mixed nuts (almonds, cashews, walnuts)
- Olives, cornichons
- Fig jam, apricots
- Fresh flowers for decor
- La Panzanella crackers (rustic, artisan-looking crackers)
- Fruit and nut crostini crackers
- Candied orange slices

Erin's Top 3 Tips for Your
Fall Cheese and Charcuterie Board

Think about how the platter will be blended into the event or the party. Will it serve as an appetizer, the main feature of a buffet-style display, or be served as a dessert course? This will help you determine the types of things to put on the board.

Consider the colors of the season. For the fall, put a small decorative pumpkin on the platter and find some cheese leaves in autumn colors. Figs are in season in early November, and they make a beautiful presentation when sliced. If it is closer to the holidays, add pomegranate, cut persimmon slices, starfruit, candied fruits, holly sprigs, etc.

How to build your board: think of building a small city, with cheeses as the buildings, rivers of cured meats, and vegetation of fruits and vegetables for more decor. Use two or three different types of crackers . . . always something crisp, but without a lot of extra seasoning or seeds, as those can mask the true flavor of the cheese. Finally, fill in the spaces with mixed nuts and dried sour cherries or cranberries, and place herbs and flowers as the finishing artistic touches.

Note: Vacherin Mont d'Or is a cow's milk cheese made in the Swiss Alps only in the months of August through March, which makes this a very special cheese to find. When served at room temperature, it becomes an ooey, gooey, stinky cheese with softness that must be scooped up with crackers. Vacherin is a real special treat for the holidays.

If you have trouble finding it, Erin says: "There are many soft, rich and oozy washed-rind cheeses from France and the U.S. that will be great substitutes for the hard to find Vacherin."

Cracker Pairings

- Slice up a baguette
- Fruit and nut crostini crackers
- Walnut and cranberry bread
- Venture away from crackers and try something new, like pairing apples with cheddar cheese!
- If the cheese board is to be served as a dessert course, make sure you have a triple creme, a washed rind, a firm cheese, and a sweeter cheese such as an aged Gouda and, of course, a blue cheese, which can be paired with honey, jams, chocolates, and dessert wines.

Winter

WINTER IS AN AMAZING "wine season" with holiday parties, family dinners, après-ski, and romantic nights by the fire. All of these occasions are an opportunity either to indulge in rich, yummy, cold weather wines or to find that great value wine you can feel proud serving your guests without breaking the bank. These wines can range from various bottles of sparkling wine, interesting varietals, and classic big American wines that we all love.

Spectrum of Winter Wines

WHITES	REDS
Champagne	Sangiovese
Gewürztraminer	Nebbiolo (Barolo)
Gavi	Malbec
California Chardonnay	Cabernet Sauvignon
	Amarone
	Port

White Wines

CHAMPAGNE *(FRANCE)*

In the winter season there are so many occasions to serve Champagne. A bottle of bubbly Champagne is the perfect accompaniment to festive holiday toasts, New Year's Eve, and a romantic Valentine's Day. In order for this bottle of bubbles to be called Champagne, it has to be from the region of Champagne, France, where the two grapes predominant in the making of Champagne are Chardonnay and Pinot Noir. The traditional wine-making method that makes Champagne so special is called méthode traditionelle when the second fermentation process is done in the bottle. A tiny bit of yeast is added to ferment, then it's removed, which imparts the classic toasty brioche flavor to the wine.

The sweetness of Champagnes and other sparkling wines can vary. The sweeter the Champagne, the better to match with sweet desserts: think wedding cake with an Extra Dry or Demi-Sec. The dryer or less sweet Champagne makes for a magical match with many foods, especially anything creamy or fried: creamy risotto, thick chowder, light cream pasta sauce; fried chicken, fried calamari, or my favorite pairing—French fries and Champagne! I encourage you to try some very crisp French Fries (steak frites en francais) with a nice cold glass of Champagne. The bubbles cut through the fat, creating a special gastronomic delight enjoyed in many French bistros every day.

All Champagnes are best when served nice and cold, at 48°–50°F.

Champagne Styles:

- Demi-Sec—Sweet
- Sec—Off dry, between sweet and dry
- Extra Dry—Fruity
- Brut—Dry
- Extra Brut—Very dry
- Natural—Least amount of sugars

Champagne and Aging
I am talking about the bottles, not you!

I'm often asked how long to keep that special bottle of Champagne that was given as a wedding or other special gift. Champagne is typically ready to serve as soon as it is purchased because it already will have been aged at the vineyard for the appropriate length of time.

The most important part of storing these special bottles is keeping them stable and cool. If they are put in a closet or cabinet, they will most likely heat up in the summer when homes get warm, resulting in a bottle of sad, flat Champagne with no bubbles. Vintage Champagne has already been aged for at least 5–10 years before it was purchased; non-vintage will have at least three years of age on it.

Unless you are storing Champagne properly you risk the chance of it dying in the bottle. So, if you have those special bottles just waiting to be opened, there is no time like the present! If you have been properly storing vintage Champagnes and have the opportunity to enjoy them, you will notice they have a mellower effervescence and an elegant toastiness. In the younger non-vintage Champagne, you will notice a brighter effervescence and a citrus freshness.

Celebrate with Champagne and Decadence!

Believe it or not, my favorite New Year's Eve tradition has been sitting on the couch with my friend Donna. We are usually in Killington, Vermont, sitting by the fire, wearing our PJs, enjoying watching old movies (usually ones featuring Audrey Hepburn), and sipping Champagne. We indulge in shrimp cocktails, or stuffed lobster tails. Light seafood goes well with effervescent Champagne, usually a dry Blanc-de-Blanc (made with all white grapes). The bubbles are not only a way of celebrating, they also offer a perfect balance with light, delicious seafood. And you should always sip Champagne when watching Audrey Hepburn.

GEWÜRZTRAMINER
(GERMANY, FRANCE, AND ITALY)

This delicious wine offers up floral and slightly tropical fruit flavor. Predominantly known as a German varietal, Gewürztraminer is grown in France, New Zealand, Italy, Germany, Oregon, and California.

Legend has it that this grape's origin is most likely Northern Italy. Like many "later harvest" wines, Gewürztraminer has a higher alcohol content because the grapes stay on the vine longer and build up residual sugars, which give the wine a touch of sweetness, though it is not as sweet as a Moscato. This wine pairs very well with spicy foods; I also think of it as a great "take out food" wine. If you are looking for a lavish glass of white wine to cool down spicy foods like vindaloo, samosa, empanadas, or even sushi with wasabi and ginger, try Gewürztraminer. This wine has a viscosity that coats and cools your mouth from the heat of the spices. An excellent winter white, Gewürztraminer is loaded with lush lychee, tropical fruit, ginger, and rose petal aromatics.

Best when served at 45°F.

Great Wine Gift!

When you bring a gift of wine, you hope to make a good impression. Why not make it a gift that lasts longer than the party you've been invited to or a bottle that ends up in the recycling bin before sunrise? A perfect gift that will stand out from the mass of bottles presented to your host, something that will be set aside and enjoyed for weeks to come, is a bottle of Port. Elegant and rich, each time Port is poured and enjoyed by the winter fire, it will be a pleasant reminder of your thoughtfulness.

The most popular Port styles are Tawny and Ruby. I personally like them both for their differences:

- **Tawny Port** can have notes of wood, berry, and raisin, with a rich finish without being too sweet.

- **Ruby Port** has tones of deep rich honey, hazelnut, and cocoa. This Port has a heady fragrance and is lush on the palate.

I have shown both of these styles of Port at many Wine Tasting events. Guests have always commented that they are surprised how much they enjoy them. And to my surprise, when asked which style they prefer, the majority of people choose the Ruby style. I have always thought when I put these Ports side by side that the Tawny Port with its woodsy raisin warmth would be the crowd-pleaser. But, consistently the Ruby Ports, with their nutty cocoa and brighter berry flavor, have been the hit.

Aunt Sue's Seafood Casserole

I come from a family of great cooks. My mother and my aunt Sue have cooked every family holiday dinner with amazing recipes inspired by our New England family history. Aunt Sue has lived at the beach in New Hampshire my whole life, and she has always been inspired by the local fish and shellfish in her cooking. Her Seafood Casserole is so delicious and is an elegant and simple dish for your holiday table, too. Try it out!

Ingredients

- 6 Tbsp. unsalted butter
- 2 oz. white mushrooms, finely chopped
- 2 cloves garlic, finely chopped
- 1 stalk celery, finely chopped
- 1 sweet orange bell pepper, stemmed, seeded, and finely chopped
- ½ small yellow onion, finely chopped
- ½ cup dry white wine
- 4 Tbsp. flour
- 1 cup milk
- 1 cup half-and-half
- 4 oz. cooked lobster meat, cut into 1-inch pieces
- ½ pound skinless haddock or cod, pin bones removed, cut into 1-inch pieces
- ½ pound large sea scallops, thinly sliced crosswise
- 1 Tbsp. fresh lemon juice
- 1 Tbsp. country-style Dijon mustard
- Kosher salt and freshly ground black pepper, to taste
- ⅓ cup fine bread crumbs
- 3 Tbsp. grated cheddar cheese
- 1 tsp. paprika
- Parsley, roughly chopped, for garnish (optional)

Directions

- Heat oven to 400°F.

- Melt 4 Tbsp. butter in a 4-qt. saucepan over medium-high heat.

- Add mushrooms, garlic, celery, bell pepper, and onion; cook, stirring occasionally, until soft, about 8 minutes.

- Add wine; cook until liquid is reduced by half, about 3 minutes.

- Add flour; cook, stirring until smooth, for 2 minutes.

- Whisk in milk and half-and-half; bring to a boil.

- Reduce heat to medium; cook until slightly thickened, 3–4 minutes.

- Stir in lobster, haddock, scallops, lemon juice, mustard, salt, and pepper.

- Divide mixture evenly among six, 6 oz. ramekins; place ramekins on a baking sheet and set aside.

- Mix bread crumbs, cheese, and paprika in a bowl; sprinkle mixture evenly over each ramekin and dot with remaining butter.

- Bake until lightly browned and bubbling in the center, about 20 minutes. Sprinkle with parsley if you like.

CORTESE (GAVI) *(ITALY)*

Though I feature Gavi in the Fall section of whites, it bears repeating in winter! With a lot of life and body for spicy, cold weather dishes, Gavi is a favorite and famous white wine of Italy. Grown in the north and made from the Cortese grape, this Italian dinner staple wine has a punch of acidity and aromatic flavors—you might even notice a touch of almond.

If you're a Sauvigon Blanc fan but want something with a bit more body to go with your winter cuisine, Gavi is a great switch. With its enticing flavor, this wine pairs beautifully with spiced chicken dishes like tandoori, and with smoked cheeses, chicken scarpariello, and any recipes that feature cured ham.

Best when served at 45°F.

CHARDONNAY *(CALIFORNIA)*

Chardonnay is the most popular wine in the world. From its birthplace as Chablis in Burgundy, France—where it is an elegant dinner wine with warm apple and mineral flavor—to California—with its traditional barrel-oaked and buttery style, the rich, full-bodied California Chardonnays have developed a cult following here in America, a passionate group that is not easily swayed (my mom included!). These oaky butter bombs with essences of tropical notes can overpower a lot of warmer weather cuisine, but winter is the time to enjoy them with creamy risotto, roast chicken, and root vegetables.

A big mistake that many people make is serving Chardonnay really cold. When it is too cold—and I mean as cold as Sauvignon Blanc or sparkling wine should be—the extreme chill will mask the beautiful butter, oak, and peach flavors. You should remove your Chardonnay from refrigeration and let it warm up to 55°–58°F. (The average kitchen refrigerator is 42°F. Many wine refrigerators are set at 48°F.) This way you will still have a slight chill but be able to fully recognize the big flavors of California Chardonnay that you love.

Best when served at 55–58°F.

Red Wines

SANGIOVESE *(ITALY)*

Tart, fresh, and delicious, the Sangiovese grape is such a chameleon. It produces three very different wines. From this single grape varietal, grown in three different regions of Tuscany, comes completely different wines in richness, depth, and flavor.

Hands down, the succulent, purplish-black Sangiovese grape is the base that makes Chianti what it is. Sangiovese is also the main grape for Vino Nobile di Montepulciano and Brunello di Montalcino. One of the main differences among these wines is the amount of the Sangiovese grape used in production; another difference has to do with the neighborhood in Tuscany where they are grown.

Here are a few facts that depict the grape's versatility:

- **Chianti** is made of 80 percent of the Sangiovese grape and may be blended with up to 20 percent of other grapes, which may include a touch of **Cabernet** and a touch of **Merlot**.

- **Vino Nobile di Montepulciano** can be blended with up to 30 percent of other varietals.

- **Brunello di Montalcino** is strictly made with 100 percent Sangiovese grapes.

When it comes to these three wines, think Little Brother, Big Brother, Big Daddy in terms of boldness and richness in flavor. They are related, yet they are completely unique wines.

As many of us know, Chianti (my self-proclaimed Little Brother) is a classic wine found on every Italian table. Thoughts of this wine may bring up images of a straw-wrapped bottle called a fiasco. The wrapping was thought to add protection to the bottles during shipping. But make no mistake, Chianti is no fiasco. Ask for a recommendation next time you dine at your favorite Italian restaurant. I'm sure you will agree that this elegant, flavorful wine stands up perfectly to rich, hearty Italian fare. Sangiovese offers a wide range of tastes from very earthy and rustic—as is the case with many Chianti Classico varieties—to round and fruit-forward.

Vino Nobile di Montepulciano (our Big Brother) is a wine made from Sangiovese grapes grown in Montepulciano—a hill town located in a region about 25 miles southeast of Siena, in southeastern Tuscany. The grapes grown in the hills are cooler at night, which adds a brighter acidity to the grapes. Vino Nobile di Montepulciano has rich, red fruits and a touch of spice.

Brunello di Montalcino is a delicious wine, the Big Daddy of them all. It hails from a Tuscan hill town that is thought to have first been settled in 900 BC. This is a big wine, full of complexity, power, and the ripe, rich flavors of cherry, fig, anise, and floral notes. Brunello di Montalcino wines are made of 100 percent Sangiovese grapes, and truly show off the full expression of what this grape can be.

**All wines from the Sangiovese grape
are best served at 58–60°F.**

Bonus Party Tip!
Tempranillo

You've set the date and sent out the invites. Now, what do you serve your crowd? We all want to make sure our guests have a great time enjoying the food and wine. But there's no reason why you can't stay within a reasonable budget. Whether you're creating charcuterie boards or serving savory hors d'oeuvres, you can provide crowd-pleaser wines from Spain, such as Rioja. Made from the Tempranillo grape, Rioja is from the famous region of La Rioja in northern Spain, which is known for wines with flavors of dark berries, herbs, and a touch of tobacco. With medium tannins and acidity, Rioja pairs well with heavier cheeses and dried meats. If you're serving chili at your party or another rich winter dish, this choice is a real crowd-pleaser.

NEBBIOLO *(BAROLO)*

Nebbiolo is the sexy Italian cousin to Pinot Noir. This medium-bodied red wine originates in the mountains of northern Italy. The deep-garnet-colored grapes produce bright, dancing tannins that leave notes of plump berries on the tongue. Don't be fooled by the delicate scent— the wine has a surprisingly hearty tannin and high acidity. The Nebbiolo grapes date back to the 13th century; they are highly sought after for resulting in some of the finest wines in Italy. Grown in the Barolo region of Piedmont, these special grapes make beautiful dinner wines, and they are also the basis of all great Barolos. Nebbiolo is ideal to enjoy with dried meats, rich pasta dishes, butternut squash, roasted garlic and fennel, and full-flavored cheese.

Best when served at 58–60°F.

MALBEC *(FRANCE)*

Malbec from Argentina is incredibly popular and has a fun history. When that region of the world had vineyards planted, the grapes were brought to South America from France. Some wine historians believe the intention of these early winemakers was to bring Merlot vines there. Surprise! They realized after the vines were planted and established that they had actually brought Malbec vines. And good thing they did, as these vines flourished in their country.

Malbec is grown in France, where it is blended into Bordeaux wine. But it is mostly famed for its bold, spicy, fruit-filled wines from Argentina where 70 percent of the Malbec varietal worldwide is grown. Malbec is a juicy fruit-forward wine with hearty plum and blackberry notes. Most Cabernet snobs find themselves extremely attracted to this wine. Rich in body, flavor, and nice acidity, Malbec ages into a velvety lush wine.

Enjoy Malbec with holiday roast lamb or roast duck, with sweet cherry sauce, or with charcuterie boards and steaks on the grill.

I especially love serving Malbec with my garlic pork roast. I make a delicious sauce (recipe follows) to drizzle on top. I have also included my favorite recipe for beef stew (yes, it's authentic!).

Best when served at 58°–60°F.

Sliced Pork Sauce

Ingredients

- 1 cup orange juice
- ½ cup soy sauce
- 2 Tbsp. honey

Directions

Mix all ingredients and reduce in a sauce pan on low heat. Drizzle on top of sliced pork roast or on pork tenderloin.

Mimi's Beef Stew

My great-great-grandmother, Hanna, came to America from Ireland. She brought with her a strand of pearls given to her by her father, which I proudly have, a wooden rocking chair, that my mother has featured in her home, and her recipe for beef stew. My mother, Donna, otherwise known to my boys as Mimi, has made this stew my whole life. When the cold weather arrives in New Hampshire, this remains a staple meal in our house. Served with warm rolls, it reminds me of coming home from sledding with my friends, dropping my wet mittens and boots, and diving into a delicious bowl. I usually make a double batch and freeze half. And I now often serve it to family and friends with a nice Malbec.

Mimi's Beef Stew

Ingredients

- 2 lbs. sirloin beef cut into 1-inch pieces
- 3 Tbsp. flour
- 2 cans beef consommé, plus 3 cans water
- 3 Tbsp. butter
- 1 tsp olive oil
- salt and pepper
- 1 lb. small red potatoes, cut into bite-size pieces
- 1 large sweet onion, chopped
- 3 garlic cloves, chopped
- 6–8 carrots, peeled and sliced
- 1 stalk celery, chopped

- 1 medium purple top turnip, peeled and cut into bite-size pieces
- 1 Tbsp. Worcestershire sauce
- 1 sprig fresh rosemary
- ½ cup chopped fresh flat-leaf parsley

Directions

Preheat oven to 350°F. Heat large heavy pan or Dutch oven over medium-high heat; add one tsp. of olive oil and 3 Tbsp. butter. Coat the beef cubes with salt, pepper, and flour; add the beef to the pan and sear on all sides. Add onion and beef consommé; add remaining vegetables, 3 (consommé) cans of water, Worcestershire sauce, garlic, rosemary, and parsley. Stir, and cover. If using a Dutch oven, cook for 1½ hours in the preheated oven. Otherwise, simmer on the stovetop for 1½ hours, stirring occasionally. Serve with crusty bread and a delicious Malbec.

CABERNET SAUVIGNON *(FRANCE, CALIFORNIA, AND NOW IN COUNTRIES GALORE!)*

Cabernet Sauvignon is absolutely the most popular red wine in the world. Its birthplace is Bordeaux, where a cross between Sauvignon Blanc and Cabernet Franc gave birth to Cabernet Sauvignon. Whether you prefer your Cabernet Sauvignon from the traditional, elegant style of Bordeaux or the big, juicy new world "Cabs" of California, this rich and fruity wine with perky tannins has become the staple of steak dinners and fireside sipping.

But everyone knows everything about Cabernet Sauvignon, right? Answer: Probably, since it's often called "the most famous red wine grape on planet Earth." For the few who don't, here's some trivia: The grapes have thick, black skins and are grown in almost every country that produces wine; the hearty vines flourish in a wide range of climates from Canada to Australia, from Chile to Lebanon. (I bet you suspected it was only grown in France and California.) When the grapes are grown in cooler areas, the wine takes is "tighter," which is a snobby wine term that means it has a brighter flavor with an herbal quality. In warmer climates, Cabernet grapes grow into more "roundness" with heavier fruit flavor like a dark, fruity jam. So now you know!

Best when served at 55°F.

Après-Ski Dinner in the Mountains

I'm the mother of two competitive alpine ski racers. So, to say the least, I spend my winters in the mountains. We have grown our beloved "ski family" over the years. Part of what we look forward to all weekend is enjoying our multifamily potluck dinners on Saturday nights. These dinners consist of large, filling meals for tired skiers and lots of laughter (and a few of the racers' complaints about that day's race, too). Anyone who has hit the slopes can tell you that après-ski food is comfort food, especially when you are feeding racers. Athletes need carbs, protein, and fat to power through the next day. One of the most popular meals we serve is a New England favorite called American Chop Suey. Both of my sons, Chase and Brice, love this dish that's made with ground beef, green peppers, tomato sauce, and macaroni.

If you're wondering what beverage you might want to offer the adults après-ski, you can always count on Cabernet Sauvignon. It is the classic après-ski wine. Picture yourself sitting by the fire, all warm and cozy, enjoying a glass of Cabernet Sauvignon and a big bowl of American Chop Suey with your best friends. The following recipe is a Guibord family favorite; we all grew up with it.

American Chop Suey for Après-Ski

Ingredients

- 1½ lbs. grass-fed ground beef, 90% lean
- 1 tsp. oregano
- crushed red pepper (to taste)
- ½ tsp. garlic powder
- 3 Tbsp. tomato paste
- 1 cup diced onion
- 1 cup diced green pepper
- 1 stick celery, diced
- ½ cup chopped mushrooms
- 4 cloves garlic, minced
- 16 oz. whole San Marzano tomatoes, crushed by hand, including the juice
- 6 oz. dry red wine
- 8 oz. tomato sauce
- 1 lb. elbow macaroni, uncooked
- ½ cup grated Parmesan

Directions

Brown beef in a large pot over medium heat until cooked through. Drain the fat from the meat (if needed). Add onions, garlic, peppers, mushrooms, celery, and spices; sauté about 5 minutes until the vegetables soften. Stir in tomato paste. Add the whole tomatoes that you have broken down by hand. Add the red wine, tomato sauce, and ¼ cup grated Parmesan. Simmer. Boil the macaroni and drain, mix with the beef mixture, add the remaining Parmesan and serve (with Cabernet Sauvignon, of course!).

AMARONE *(ITALY)*

Oh Amarone, I love you so! This is the most romantic and sexy wine. This red wine is made in an extremely special way. A blend of traditional Valpolicella grapes (Corvina, Rondinella, Corvinone, and Oseleta) are harvested in October, and then placed on grass mats or racks to semi-dry until January. During this process, the grapes lose about 50 percent of their weight and the level of natural sugar is concentrated. The intensity in the flavor of the semi-dried grapes is what makes this wine so spectacular: think black cherry, brown sugar, and chocolate.

You may experience some sticker shock when you see the prices of these amazing Amarones. Because of the months-long drying time for the grapes, you can imagine how many more are needed to make just one bottle of wine. The lush dried fruit and mocha flavor provides a heady experience to be enjoyed with roast lamb, rich ragu sauce, and especially with full-flavored cheese and dark chocolate. This is a very special bottle that I always recommend for anniversary celebrations, special holiday dinners, and romantic evenings.

Best when served at 58–60°F.

Amarone: The Perfect Winter Romance Wine

Though the Italian word for "love" is amore, *in Spanish "to love" is* amar. *Close enough, right? Amarone, after all, is a big, romantic red wine that calls for a cozy winter night by the fire with that special someone and lots of love!*

PORT *(PORTUGAL)*

The name for this wine—which dates back to the late 16th century—derived from the city of Oporto in Douro Valley of northern Portugal, where the Douro River meets the Atlantic Ocean. Thanks to the guidelines of the European Union Protected Designation of Origin, wines from Portugal are the only ones that can legally be labeled "Port."

As I mentioned earlier, a good Port is my top choice to present to your favorite hosts and hostesses.

(See: **Great Wine Gift!**) Because we all put so much of our own personal style and pocketbook into selecting a wine to give, my solution is simple: bring a bottle of Port. This beautiful wine can be sipped after dinner with a dessert or rich cheese. If you're going to present it to wine lovers, most likely they don't think to buy a bottle of Port for themselves, but would enjoy having one.

The wine for Port is produced and then fortified with a neutral spirit made from the skins and stems of the grapes, which makes the alcohol content much higher, thus preserving the wine for longer. So, when your lucky recipients open the bottle, they can enjoy this bottle for months to come and be reminded of you, your savvy wine expertise, and your clever generosity. And Port isn't just for parties: it's a great holiday gift idea that slides nicely into a red-and-white fuzzy stocking! (Did you hear that, Santa?)

Best when served at 55°F.

Valentine's Day

Whether you have a Valentine's or "Galentines" Day celebration, it's a chance to cherish your relationships and celebrate love in general. It is also an opportunity (or an excuse!) to indulge in some great wine! It can be easier than you think to create a gift (or experience) that seems custom-made for your loved one. A fun idea can be to personalize your gift. For a bottle of wine, you can print out a custom label that has greater meaning, such as an inside joke or a photograph from your childhood. There are many vendors online who will custom-make wine labels that vary from funny and silly to romantic. Get creative! You can even send one to your Ex.

Don't like a crowded dining room on Valentine's Day? Another thought is to take it easy and dine in. A great option is to pair Gewürztraminer with Chinese take-out.

Break the Rules for Chocolate!

Everyone loves chocolate on Valentine's Day. And while I suggest you match your wines with your seasons throughout this book, I am now suggesting you break the rules *(just this once!)*. Here's a chocolate and wine pairing guide that will help you pair the best wines with the chocolate treats you love:

- Milk Chocolate—Sparkling Wine, Pinot Noir
- Raspberry Truffles—Syrah, Grenache
- Dark Chocolate Bark—Zinfandel, Syrah, Amarone
- Chocolate-Covered Pretzels—Pinot Noir, Cabernet Sauvignon
- Chocolate-Covered Almonds—Cabernet Sauvignon, Nebbiolo
- Peanut Butter Cups—Cabernet Sauvignon, Pinot Noir
- Dark Chocolate with Dried Fruit—Tawny Port, Zinfandel
- Milk Chocolate with Caramel—Brunello, Cabernet Sauvignon, Amarone
- Crispy Hazelnut Truffles—Malbec, Sparkling Wine
- Sea Salt Caramels—Pinot Noir, Sparkling Wine
- Chocolate Toffee—Pinot Noir, Malbec
- Chocolate-Covered Strawberries—Merlot, Sparkling Wine
- Cherry Cordials—Ruby Port, Sparkling Wine

What, Where, and Wine
Winter

- Après-ski—Champagne, Cabernet Sauvignon
- Holiday dinner party—Chardonnay, Nebbiolo, Amarone
- Gift of wine—Port (Tawny or Ruby)
- Romantic fireside sippers—Amarone, Pinot Grigio
- Cozy movie night-in—Nero d'Avola, Pinot Grigio
- New Year's Eve—Sparkling Wine from U.S., Spain, or France
- Hallmark Christmas Movies—Syrah, Pinot Grigio
- Holiday shopping—Champagne
- Pasta parties—Chianti, Gavi
- Super Bowl watching—American Zinfandel, American Chardonnay
- Bowl of chili by the fire—Nero d'Avola, Chianti

Sandra's Sipping Quiz
FOR BOOK CLUBS!

Most book clubs serve wine, so *wine not* make this book your book club selection? Here are some questions for you and your friends to go over and see what you've learned along the way.

1. Which romantic wine lays its grapes out on a mat to semi-dry in the sun?

2. Which white wine hails from the Loire Valley of France?

3. What does the term "varietal" mean?

4. How do winemakers refer to the various neighborhoods where their wines are made?

5. When we refer to Groovy Jetliner, what is the wine we are talking about?

6. Describe the wine experiment that Sandra did with her friend Ernie.

7. What happens when you put wine in a blender?

8. What is American Chop Suey and where does it originally hail from?

9. What is the most food-friendly red wine?

10. What is the name of the cheese that Sandra claims has changed her life?

11. Instead of a lunch box, what does Sandra buy each fall?

12. What is the difference between Shiraz and Syrah?

13. How many fermentation processes are there in Champagne?

14. Prosecco is made with which grape?

15. What's the difference in the aging process of Sauvignon Blanc and Fumé Blanc?

16. Which Italian wine could help you live to be 100?

17. Which green summer wine is like a spritzer in a bottle?

18. Which Italian grape could also be the name of a leading man in a romance novel?

19. What temperature is best for sparkling wine?

20. At what temperature should you serve California Chardonnays?

21. What is the primary grape in Chianti?

22. What sweet pink wine was created by mistake?

23. What are the two parent grapes for Cabernet Sauvignon?

24. What grape makes Sancerre wine?

25. Where is the birthplace of Chardonnay?

26. When someone says a wine exhibits terroir, what do they mean?

27. Which light white wine has a wisp of smoke?

28. Name a big, bad BBQ wine.

29. At what temperature should you serve Pinot Noir?

30. How has this book changed your wine identity?

ANSWER KEY

1. Which romantic wine lays its grapes out on a mat to semi-dry in the sun?
   Amarone.

2. Which white wine hails from the Loire Valley of France?
   Sancerre.

3. What does the term "varietal" mean?
   The type of grape.

4. How do winemakers refer to the various neighborhoods where their wines are made?
   Appellation.

5. When we refer to Groovy Jetliner, what is the wine we are talking about?
   Grüner Veltliner.

6. Describe the wine experiment that Sandra did with her friend Ernie.
   They did a wine oxidation challenge by tasting affordable wines that they opened and exposed to air for different periods.

7. What happens when you put wine in a blender?
   It aerates it and changes the flavor.

8. What is American Chop Suey and where does it originally hail from?
   American Chop Suey is ground beef and pasta comfort food from New England.

9. What is the most food-friendly red wine?
   Pinot Noir.

10. What is the name of the cheese that Sandra claims has changed her life?
    Coupole.

11. Instead of a lunch box, what does Sandra buy each fall?
    A new purse.

12. What is the difference between Shiraz and Syrah?
    There is no difference. They are the same grape grown in different countries.

13. How many fermentation processes are there in Champagne?
    Two.

14. Prosecco is made with which grape?
    Glera.

15. What's the difference in the aging process of Sauvignon Blanc and Fumé Blanc?
    Sauvignon Blanc is aged in steel and Fumé Blanc is aged in oak.

16. Which Italian wine could help you live to be 100?
    Vermento.

17. Which green summer wine is like a spritzer in a bottle?
    Vinho Verde.

18. Which Italian grape could also be the name of a leading man in a romance novel?
    Nero d'Avola.

19. What temperature is best for sparkling wine?
    45°F.

20. At what temperature should you serve California Chardonnays?

    55°F.

21. What is the primary grape in Chianti?

    Sangiovese.

22. What sweet pink wine was created by mistake?

    White Zinfandel.

23. What are the two parent grapes for Cabernet Sauvignon?

    Cabernet Franc and Sauvignon Blanc.

24. What grape makes Sancerre wine?

    Sauvignon Blanc.

25. Where is the birthplace of Chardonnay?

    Burgundy, France.

26. When someone says a wine exhibits terroir, what do they mean?

    The wine tastes the way the wine is grown and the variations that make it special from region to region.

27. Which light white wine has a wisp of smoke?

    Pouilly-Fumé.

28. Name a big, bad BBQ wine.

    Petite Syrah or Zinfandel.

29. At what temperature should you serve Pinot Noir?
     55°F.

30. How has this book changed your wine identity?

_____

_____

_____*!*

Acknowledgments

IF I TRIED TO WRITE THIS BOOK on my own, I would have had no fun at all! So, what do you do when you have a big project to accomplish? You look around you and see all the talent and skills of your friends, bribe them with wine, and poof! You magically have an amazing team!

My all-star team starts with my editor, Jean Stone. She held my hand, gave me amazing advice on how to collect my stories, and assured me that this would be a fantastic journey. Not only did I learn so much from her, but she also became my friend, for which I am grateful.

Sarah Galluzzo jumped in with verve, acuity, and her silly puns. What fun we had together! Things moved along quickly with her cleverness, style, and mad organizational writing. We sipped some good wine along the way, too.

Jillian Stevens came on board the Sandra's Wine Life team and has become a valuable driving force. Her positive heart and tenacity are infectious!

I have known photographer John Fortunato since my early teenage days as a model. I am thrilled that we had the chance to reconnect, and that his beautiful photography is throughout my book.

My heartfelt gratitude to all my friends and family that I have spent my life cooking, laughing, traveling, and sipping wine with. These are only a fraction of the amazing memories I have of so many wonderful times together.

CPSIA information can be obtained
at www.ICGtesting.com
Printed in the USA
JSHW030222301122
34084JS00007B/70

9 781935 052852